To
JAN
READ, DIG… …EW,

HAPPY BIRT…
F

START DRESSMAKING

A book for beginners

Ann Ladbury

Dryad Press Ltd London

DEDICATION

This book is for Charlotte Orba and all the other young sewers I know

METRIC CONVERSION CHART

(approximate)

3mm	1/8in
6mm	1/4in
1cm	3/8in
2cm	3/4in
3cm	1 1/8in
4cm	1 5/8in
5cm	2in
6cm	2 3/8in
7cm	2 3/4in
8cm	3 1/8in
9cm	3 1/2in
10cm	4in
20cm	7 7/8in
30cm	11 7/8in
40cm	15 3/4in
50cm	19 5/8in
100cm	39 3/8in

Diagram patterns on pages 49, 60 and 70 give measurements for size 10 with size 12 in brackets where appropriate.

First published 1986

ISBN 0 8521 9683 0

Typeset by Tek-Art Ltd, Kent
and printed in Great Britain by
Anchor Brendon Ltd
Tiptree, Essex
for the publishers
Dryad Press Ltd.
8 Cavendish Square
London W1M 0AJ

CONTENTS

INTRODUCTION

There are lots of reasons for wanting to learn to sew. The motivation may be the desire to wear something individual or the result of frustration at not finding what you want ready-made; for many people the desire begins with looking at displays of attractive fabrics; for others it is simply the need to be creative.

Whatever the reason for learning to sew the enthusiasm of the beginner can be quickly dampened if success is not soon forthcoming. Beginners are liable to make mistakes but they haven't the experience to know how to rescue the project by correcting the errors and converting it to a success. Success is easily measured; clothes have to be worn. When the first attempts are worn, even bringing admiring comments from others, a beginner has the confidence to go on to make something else. If not, things are likely to be hidden away unfinished and unless help is available the beginner may be unwilling to try again for fear of encountering the same problems.

It is important for you to build up confidence along with practical skills by attempting only those articles that are within your capabilities and which you know you have time to complete.

Starting to sew involves learning about a number of things. Long before the skills of construction are tackled there are some decisions to be made concerning what to make, what fabric to use and what equipment will be needed. Many people are familiar with some of the basic equipment, perhaps as a result of making curtains or doing repairs, but they have no knowledge of fabrics or sewing aids. Some people have no experience at all. It helps if you familiarise yourself with all these things by spending some time in fabric and haberdashery departments. Look at the fabrics, feel them, read the labels, discover the variety of different widths as well as looking at designs. Look at sewing tools and haberdashery and read the instructions; look through the pattern catalogues to see what styles and sizes are available. Then, when you are ready to buy, plan a leisurely shopping trip so that you can take your time making a choice.

This book explains what is involved in making clothes, how to go about it, what to make, what you need and how to perform the basic operations; it provides the groundwork and it gives you a plan from which to work. Use it as a springboard to go on to more ambitious projects; use it as a reference book for basic techniques even when you have progressed beyond the need for the simple explanations.

Using the book will inspire confidence in beginners by offering projects and tips which guarantee success and once you start to build up experience you will sense the satisfaction of having a craft at your finger tips that you will enjoy for life.

Clothes are made by cutting fabric (material) into shapes and joining them together to make a different shape, one that fits and flatters the body. The more complex the final article, the more pieces of fabric there will be and so the longer it will take to put together and, usually, the more skill will be needed to do it. Beginners, therefore, should select things made from only a few pieces of fabric to be joined to form a simple shape. The pieces have to be cut to an exact size, either from a commercially produced paper pattern or by following an outline drawn in a magazine or book. Those drawn in books are referred to as diagram patterns.

A paper pattern is made from tissue on which shapes are printed; these are cut out and used as templates for cutting fabric. Diagram-patterns are drawn small scale and have to be scaled up to full size. This can be done on sheets of paper which are then cut and used as templates, or, with simple things, the paper can be dispensed with and the shapes drawn directly onto the fabric. Either form of pattern is satisfactory provided the terms and descriptions used in the written text can be understood. In this book there are several designs shown as diagram-patterns; following these and making the articles will provide the necessary experience for following other diagram-patterns you may use. Also, reading the chapter in this book on commercially-produced tissue patterns will simplify their use sufficiently for a beginner to make something successfully.

1
WHAT TO MAKE

Make something similar to a favourite item already in your wardrobe. This way you will know how it will look when it is finished. One disadvantage of making your own clothes is that you often do not know what the finished effect will be until it is nearly complete. The latest fashion trend may not suit you; find out if it does by trying on ready-made clothes before you rush off and buy a pattern. Always make something you know you will wear; for example don't make trousers if you don't normally wear them.

Decide on something in a medium-weight fabric; not fur or coating, not chiffon or georgette but something in-between like cotton. Choose loose styles with very few techniques: choose tops rather than blouses; choose wrap-over things and simple dresses that pull over the head.

Go for: raglan or all-in-one sleeves; elastic or drawstring waists; unpressed pleats rather than set pleats; pull-on trousers and shorts with elastic waists and, if you are making for children, choose simple shapes.

For a while avoid: time-consuming processes and those requiring experience such as: zips, collars, buttonholes, fancy pockets, edges and frills. When you have made a few simple things progress to something that includes only one of those features.

INTEGRATE

Plan to make something that will become part of a complete outfit: it is a mistake to make an odd skirt that you then cannot wear attractively. But don't plan to make a whole outfit; it will take too long. Select something from your wardrobe, trousers, shirt or jacket to provide the basis of the outfit, plan to make one thing such as a top or wrap-over skirt to go with it and when you buy the fabric buy a co-ordinating scarf, belt, sweater or buy the yarn to knit a jacket, hat or long scarf. Keep the knitting going alongside the sewing so that they are finished together. You will be able to machine the seams in the knitting because by that time you will have mastered the sewing machine. You will find some of the processes like sewing on buttons apply to sewing and also to knitting so that learning in one craft will be of benefit to another.

WHERE TO SEW

Try to find a corner of the home where you can sew and then leave the sewing there between sessions. The greatest deterrent to sewing is the thought of having to get everything out of the cupboard. The best place to sew is in the living room, where you won't miss out on the family activities, or in the kitchen where you have handy power-points and water. It also gives other members of the family an opportunity of learning. Try not to isolate yourself in a chilly spare bedroom.

SHOPPING

Ask your friends which is the most helpful department store or shop to visit for fabric and patterns. As a beginner you don't want a confusing variety of choice but you do want helpful, patient assistants. Try and choose one with a coffee shop where you can go and think and try and make up your mind what to buy. Go early in the morning before they get busy so that you can ask for advice; there will be room to stand back and look at fabric too. If you have already got your pattern or a diagram-pattern take it with you, ask if you can lay it out on the fabric on the counter.

If you have no one to advise you on what is easy and what is difficult, the following lists will prove useful.

Easy	*Difficult*
Cotton	Thick fabric
Cotton jersey	Heavy fabric

Other types of jersey except very thick
Thin towelling
Light-weight wool
Fabric that doesn't fray
Sundress with straps
Camisole top
Anything that wraps and ties
Culottes
Plain necklines
Separates
Sleeves with gathered tops
Pockets in seams
Skirts that eliminate the zip by wrapping over the pocket

Tailored clothes
Shirtwaist dress
Fitted clothes
Collars
Lapels
Shirt collars
Dress with sleeves
Stitching on the outside
Pleats
Fly zips
Openings
Sleeve openings
Buttoned cuffs

STORAGE

Invest in a cabinet with drawers for your machine. Many cabinets take most makes of machine, or alternatively, can be adapted to specification. The machine can be left out between sessions and will not be in the way of family meals, or you can quickly tidy things away and close it up. If you don't wish to start with a cabinet, a second-hand desk is a good substitute. Buy a swivel stool which can be adjusted to the correct height for you when machining. You can swing round to reach things or to use an adjacent surface and it is easier to get on and off than a chair.

Buy a cutting and sewing board on which to work; open it out on the dining table to prevent scratches and use it to move your sewing without disturbing it. You can also use it on the bed or on the floor. When cutting-out spread out the fabric using the lines on the board for keeping edges straight. Use the diagonal lines to cut crossway strips, cut straight edges for extra things like belts using the vertical lines on the board. Use the board for sewing – tacking and lining up edges – and, when in an armchair to do hand-sewing, trimming, etc. have the board folded across your lap.

For storing your sewing and haberdashery use polythene bags of various sizes. A selection of boxes is also useful. Those that come in sets with a transparent panel at one end can be piled up in a cupboard or in the wardrobe and you can

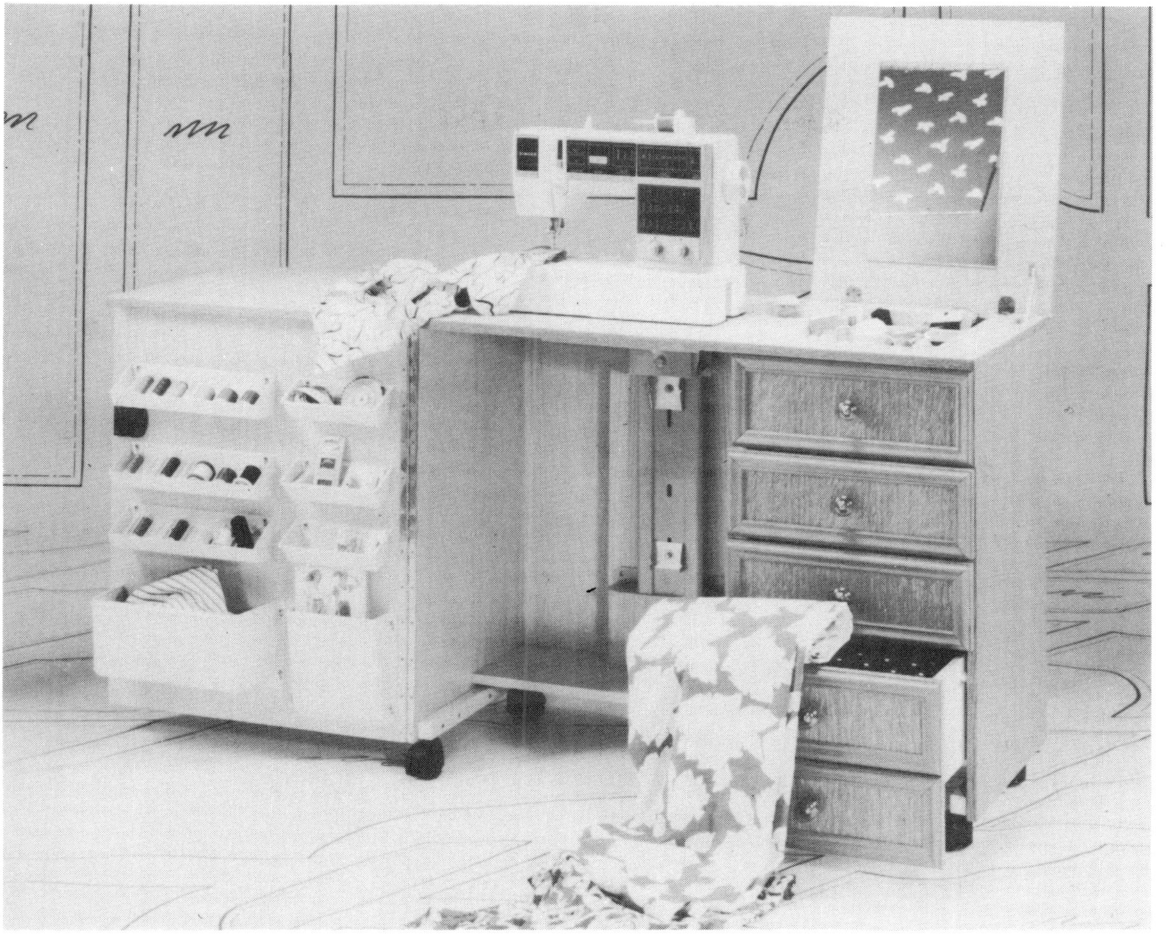

fig. 1. The Singer Sewing Centre *combines good storage room with extensive workspace. Photograph by courtesy of Singer Consumer Product Division*

easily see what each contains. Some items of office equipment can also be useful; consider plastic containers and stacked filing trays for example. If you have to sew in the livingroom buy a sheet of gardener's plastic sheeting to spread over the carpet around the machine. Most important of all, have a large waste-paper bin beside you whenever you sew.

2
FABRICS

Fabric is manufactured flat and then rolled, or, alternatively, folded along its length and then rolled up. This is how it is displayed in shops, although a selection of fabrics is usually unrolled and displayed, sometimes even made into clothes to present an impression of how they will look when made up.

Fabrics are made in widths that vary according to the loom used. There are several commonly found standard widths and a few others that you might come across. The amount of material you need to buy differs according to the width of the fabric you choose. It is sometimes wasteful to use certain widths and this depends on the size of the pattern pieces. The aim is to cut the pieces in such a way as to leave as few wasted scraps as possible.

Fabrics are usually: approximately 90cm wide (sometimes 89cm wide or even 92cm wide),
115cm wide (or 114-116cm),
140cm wide (or 137cm),
150cm wide or
160cm wide.

Fabric is either plain colour or a woven pattern such as stripes or it is printed with a design. Fabric is either knitted or woven.

PATTERNED FABRICS

Woven and knitted fabrics may have a design printed on the right side and on good quality fabrics the design will be almost as clear on the underside. When selecting fabric remember that any crooked stitching you might do will probably not show on a printed fabric but will be obvious on a plain one. Tartans and checks are difficult to use because they must match exactly at all the seams. They should be avoided until you are experienced at sewing and can concentrate on matching the pattern.

Easy fabrics for beginners are those which are not too thin and not too thick and with a fairly small all-over design printed on one side. Alternatively, an even-striped fabric in a pale colour with white is excellent because the stripes can be used as guide lines. Another easy type of fabric is one with a border design along one edge since the border too can be used as a guide. Avoid diagonal stripes and designs that give an impression of being diagonal when seen from a distance. Also avoid any very large prints because they have to be carefully placed on the garment and this requires some experience.

WOVEN FABRICS

Woven fabric is made by interlacing yarns manufactured from a variety of fibres or mixtures of different fibres. A straightforward interweaving of a width-ways thread (called weft) over and under those running lengthwise (called warp) results in a plain weave (fig. 2). Different arrangements of weaving result in different patterns, for example herring-bone, twill and satin (fig. 3). It helps to recognise them as the

fig. 2.

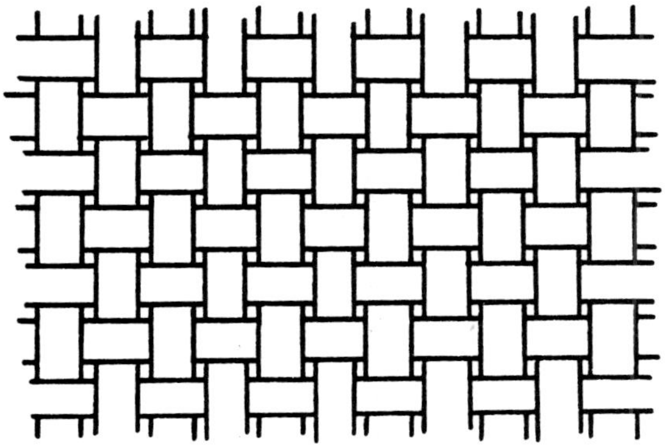

fig. 3.

weave can affect handling. You will acquire knowledge of different weaves by sewing on different fabrics.

Woven fabrics can be soft or firm, thin or thick, smooth, shiny, matt, woolly, curly, and they can be heavy enough for a thick coat or light enough for a sheer blouse.

The type of fibre and thickness of yarn determines the fabric properties.

To produce checks, tartans, stripes and other geometric effects, the yarns are dyed in various colours and then woven to a design. The effect can be seen on both sides of the fabric though often not as sharply on the underside.

KNITTED FABRICS

Knitted fabric, also called jersey, is produced on knitting machines using a continuous length of yarn (fig. 4). The resulting fabric has a distinct right side. It may also be brushed or looped. Knitted fabrics will stretch when pulled but they should spring back.

fig. 4.

3

CUTTING OUT

EQUIPMENT

Cutting out shears (buy or borrow)
Tailor's chalk (buy)
Ruler
Tape measure Buy one marked on both sides. Those marked off in colour every 10cm are the easiest to use.
Pins Buy a small box of dressmaker's steel pins. Keep them only for sewing and keep them in the box. Do not let needles get mixed in with pins.

Pins with coloured heads are easy to find in the fabric and on the floor but due to the shape of the heads they are a little more difficult to insert accurately.

HOW TO CUT FABRIC

Whatever sort of pattern you use, the fabric must be cut with care. This technique, cutting out, is not difficult if you use the right equipment, yet it is one that frightens all beginners and a number of experienced people too. It is the fear of making a wrong cut and rendering the fabric useless that is inhibiting so do the following two things until you are more confident. Find an odd piece of fabric – an old sheet or curtain – and cut it up. Practise holding the scissors, following the advice below. Secondly, when making something and ready to cut out the fabric, get someone to check it for you to make sure it is right. In no time you will be able to cut out confidently on your own.

Using cutting-out shears

These are big scissors and the shaped handles enable the

shears to be held comfortably with your thumbs in the upper part and all four fingers below. Slide your hand in until the shape fits your palm (fig. 5). Even very large shears are easy to use and once you have tried them you will realise that you have greater control and a much more efficient squeeze than with small scissors. The blades should be long,

fig. 5.

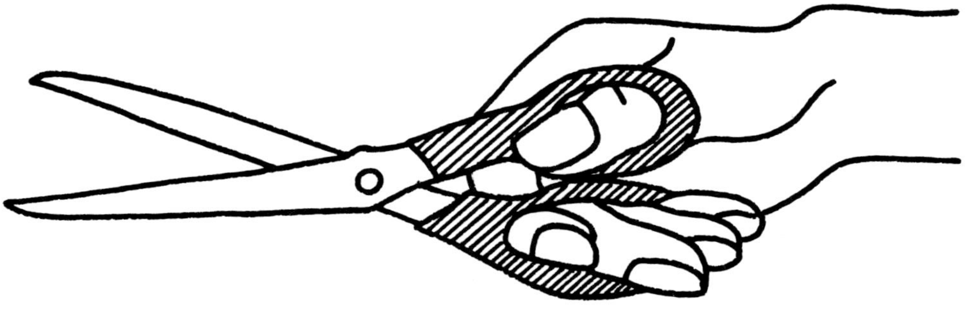

up to 25cm, and the blades bolted. If you are a beginner and haven't any shears, borrow a pair to start with and plan to buy your own once you feel confident about sewing.

Rest the scissors on the table and open the blades to a comfortable distance, slide the scissors forward over the edge of the fabric and close the scissors right to the tip. As you make a cut your eyes should move from the apex of the blades as they enclose the fabric towards the points as they close. To make a further cut open the scissors comfortably, move them forward, fit the open blade over the fabric fitting them carefully into the cut and close the scissors.

Guiding the scissors

You will need a line on which to cut and this can be made in several ways depending on what you are making. You will eventually be able to cut fabric by following the line of thread and you can practise straight lines by cutting striped fabric. Lines can be drawn on fabric using tailor's chalk as follows: sharpen the chalk by holding it vertically in one hand; open the shears and hold at the centre of the blades; shave the chalk gently on both sides to a sharp even edge; use the chalk with one edge flat on the fabric and rule away from you, using your other hand to keep the fabric flat; apply even pressure and draw firmly; use a ruler for straight lines and try making dashes on curves instead of a solid line.

If you are using a paper pattern pin it to the fabric by

placing it in the position shown in fig. 6. Insert pins well within the edge of the paper, lifting the points sharply up again as they hit the table. Use the forefinger of the other hand to ease the fabric onto the pin. Do not use too many

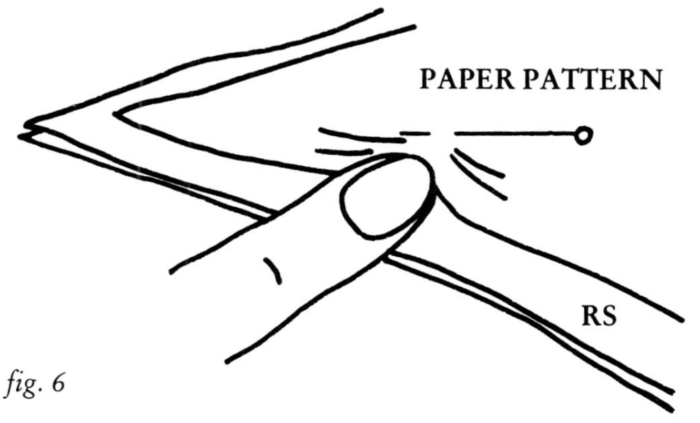

fig. 6

pins. Cut out with the pattern edge to the right so that your head is directly above the scissors. This way you avoid a chopped edge because you can see what you are doing.

Cut curves by swinging your elbow out as you close the scissors and do not close to the points. If small curves are really awkward to reach, cut around the whole piece, then pull it away from the remainder of the fabric and trim the curve.

SEAMS

Seams are used for joining pieces of fabric. There are different types for different fabrics and they can be made using a sewing machine or using a needle and thread and hand-stitching. A sewing machine is quickest but only if you are familiar with it – how to thread it, control it and alter the stitch. Hand-sewing often appeals to beginners simply because it is slower and because they feel more in control of what is happening. It is a good idea to start making a garment either entirely by hand, such as the quilted waistcoat shown on page 71 or one entirely by machine (see pages 48 and 52).

The iron is the only piece of equipment that is always used for all sewing on all types of fabric.

4

READY-MADE FEATURES

Make use of the various items you can buy, for example any of the following.

fig. 7

Lace collars (fig. 7)
These are available in a variety of styles, sometimes with matching cuffs or lace edging. Sew the garment to the point where at least the shoulder seams are joined and take it with you to the shop so that you can select a collar with a neckline that fits.

fig. 8

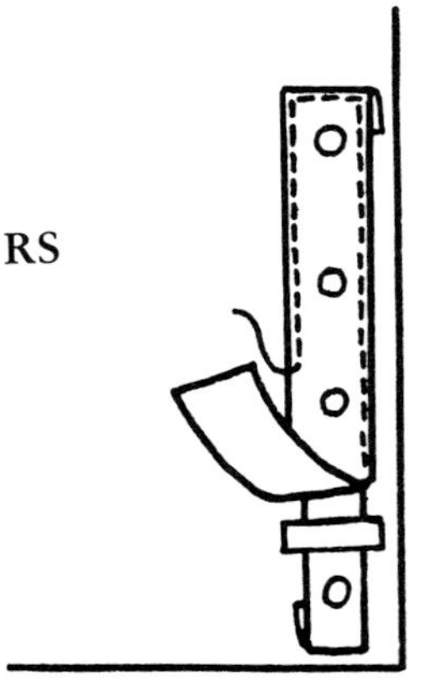

Press studs on tape (fig. 8)
These are metal studs attached at intervals to a tape which is usually white. There are two pieces of tape, one with the knobs and the other with wells attached. Use it instead of a row of hooks or buttons on the finished edge of a garment. Cut the tape to length but leave an extra 1cm to turn under. Separate the two halves of tape, place each piece in position and hold with several pieces of basting tape. Turn under the raw edge at each end and hold down. Attach the zip foot to the machine and stitch round the edge, removing the basting tape as you approach it. Fasten-off the stitching.

fig. 9

Metal eyelets (fig. 9)
Available in packs and sometimes in mixed colours and sizes. Use them as decoration or with cord or rouleau as a fastening. Buy the ones that include a special tool for attaching. Try them on spare fabric first, then mark the position of each on the garment using a fabric pen.

Metal studs with caps (fig. 10)
These can be bought in packs containing a fixing tool. Use them in place of buttons to fasten shirt fronts and cuffs,

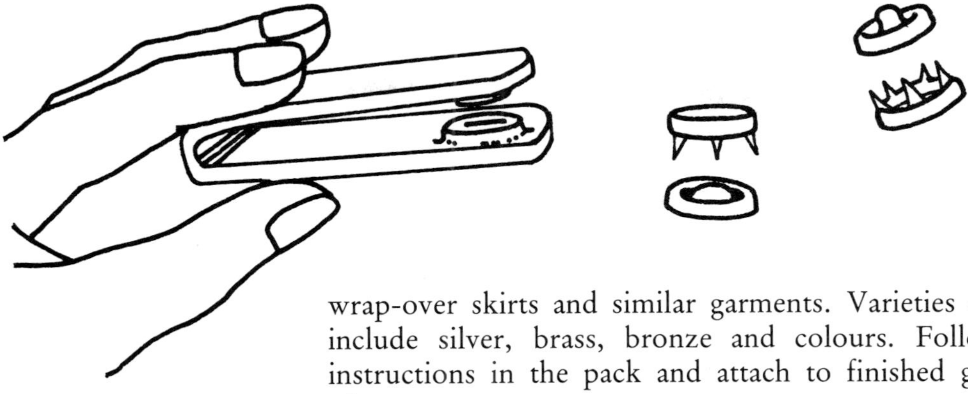

fig. 10

wrap-over skirts and similar garments. Varieties of caps include silver, brass, bronze and colours. Follow the instructions in the pack and attach to finished garment edges.

Ribbon (fig. 11)
Ribbon of all types and widths can be used and attached as for braid but it is also useful as ties instead of using fabric. Cut lengths longer than you need, turn under one end and hem firmly to the underside of the finished garment edge. Tie the ends before trimming off the surplus. Cut the ends at an angle to prevent fraying.

fig. 11

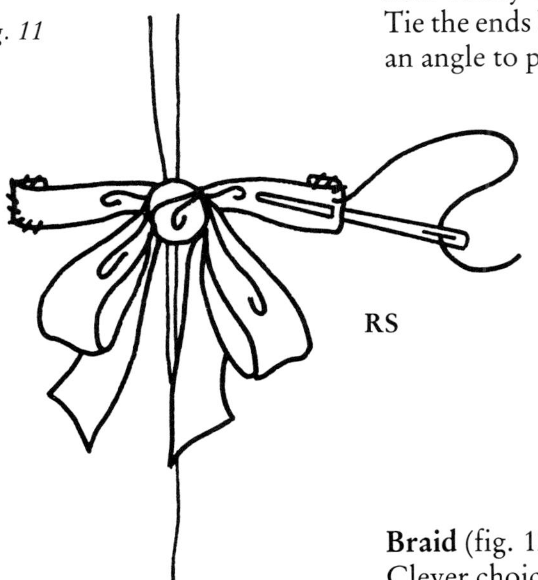

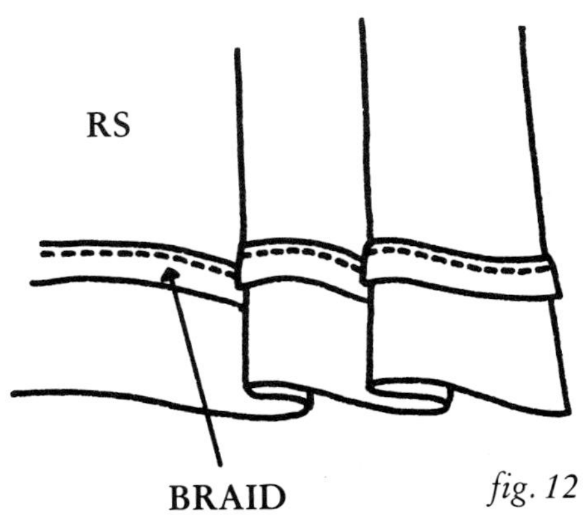

fig. 12

Braid (fig. 12)
Clever choice of braid provides instant decoration and it is a useful way of covering wobbly stitching. Attach either by using a corresponding width of Wundatrim under the braid, pressing well using a damp cloth or by machine using a small zig-zag or decorative stitch worked along each edge. When adding horizontal rows of ribbon for decoration, stitch along the upper edge only to prevent the bubbling that occurs if both edges are stitched.

Cuff and waist ribbing (fig. 13)
This is available in cut lengths which you measure round the body, wrist, waist, stretch and cut. Join the ends with a wide stretch-stitch on the machine. Join the garment seams. Hold the garment right side out and slide the ribbing over it until the raw edges are level. Ribbing for cuffs and ankles is usually already joined. Stretch the ribbing bit by bit to flatten it against the fabric and insert a few pins. Slide the garment onto the free arm of the machine with the ribbing uppermost, lower the foot between pins and stitch with a stretch stitch pulling the ribbing out flat, both behind and in front of the foot. Remove the pins as you come to them.

fig. 13

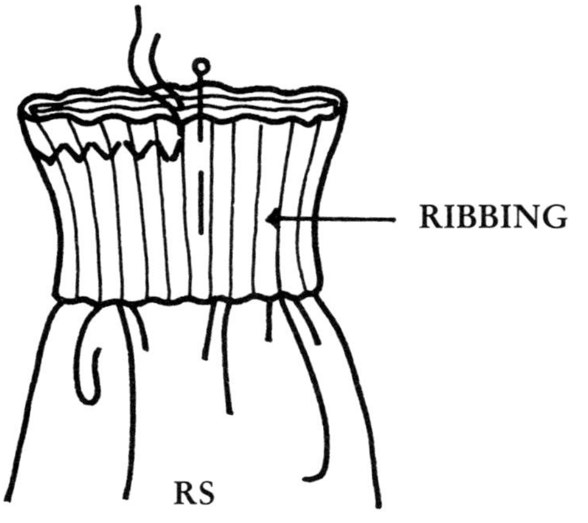

5

NEEDLE AND THREAD

The needle you use, whether for hand-sewing or machining, makes holes in the in the fabric through which the thread is drawn. It is therefore important to use a suitable size needle. One that is too thin will be difficult to use, and a machine needle which is too thin will probably break. An over-sized needle will result in large holes in the fabric and ugly stitches. The general rule is that the finer the fabric the smaller the needle for both hand and machine stitching.

MACHINE NEEDLES

There are general purpose machine needles which are used for most fabrics and additionally there are several specialist needles such as ones with spear points for sewing on leather, suede and plastic and ball point needles for knits, jersey and silky knits. It is still important to use the correct *size* of needle for the thickness of fabric.

If you are not sure whether you have the best size or type of machine needle for a fabric, listen to it. If you hear undue noise such as popping or squeaking it usually indicates that it is not a suitable needle.

fig. 14

Hand-sewing needle size	*Fabric*	*Machine-sewing needle size (Continental and English)*	*Recommended machine stitch size*
8	voile, lace, chiffon, light silks	70 9	very small straight
7	crêpe, polyester/cotton, gingham crepon, madras, poplin, taffeta	80 11	small straight
7	denim, brocade, velvet, needlecord, heavy lace, wool crêpe and challis, mohair	90 14	medium straight
6	firm wools, flannel, crêpe, curtain fabrics, corduroy, suede fabric, heavy poplin	90 14	medium straight
6	canvas, coat fabrics, tweed, fur	100 16	large straight
8	light jersey fabrics, cotton jersey, polyester knits	70 ball-point 9	small zig-zag
	sweater knits, heavy bouclé knit	90 ball-point 14	medium zig-zag
Spear point 6-7	Leather, suede, P.V.C. waterproof and plastic coated fabrics	90 14	very large

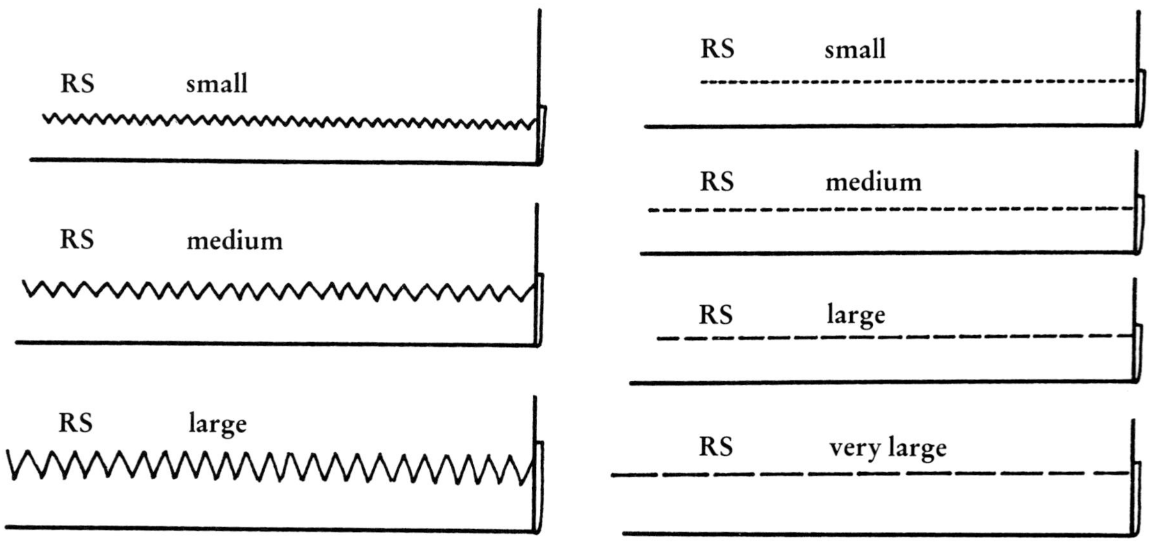

fig 15a and b.

THREAD

Drima is suitable for machining and hand-sewing on all fabrics but you need to vary the size of needle and stitch according to the fabric. See the chart on page 20 for guidance.
Drima has the following properties:
Strength and smoothness; it is fine and beds well into the fabric, it does not shrink and is rot-resistant.
Although it is one weight and one thickness it sews all fabrics from sheer to heavy and all types of synthetics and blends and all natural fibres. Probably the outstanding feature of Drima is the 'give' it has. This stretch or 'give' ensures wrinkle-free seams and it makes sure that stitching does not split in jersey fabrics or in seams subject to strain in wear.

Duet is a good general purpose sewing thread with less lustre than Drima but it may be easier to use. For instance there is no build-up of static to cause snarling or missed stitches. Duet has a core of polyester, providing strength and elasticity, and a covering of fine cotton which makes it smooth and easy to sew with.

6

BUYING AND USING A SEWING MACHINE

If you haven't a machine of your own don't rush out and buy one yet. Work through this book first, either borrowing a machine, or better still, taking your sewing to a competent friend or relation willing to be on hand while you sew. By the time you have made the clothes in this book you will be familiar with the basic operations and you could then go to a sewing machine shop to look at what is available.

WHAT TO BUY

New machines can cost £60.00 or £600.00 so the sensible thing to do is to decide what you can afford. Look at the range of operations on the machines in your price bracket. You will have discovered that it is essential to be able to zig-zag and blind hem and, later, you will want to be able to work buttonholes. Look for ease of engaging all these stitches without too much fiddling with the controls and additional feet. Make sure a zip foot is included. Some stretch stitches and a few decorative stitches are useful. Check that you can fill the bobbin easily and that you can insert it in the machine without breaking your nails. Finally, but most important, make sure you can lift the machine. Lift it off the table not from the floor. The easiest ones to carry around the house are those with the handle attached to the machine itself. There is such a wide range of machines available that you will undoubtedly find one that fulfills your requirements within your price range. Even if you can afford an advanced and sophisticated machine you would be wise to delay your choice for a while. It would be better to gain more experience on your friend's machine or even buy

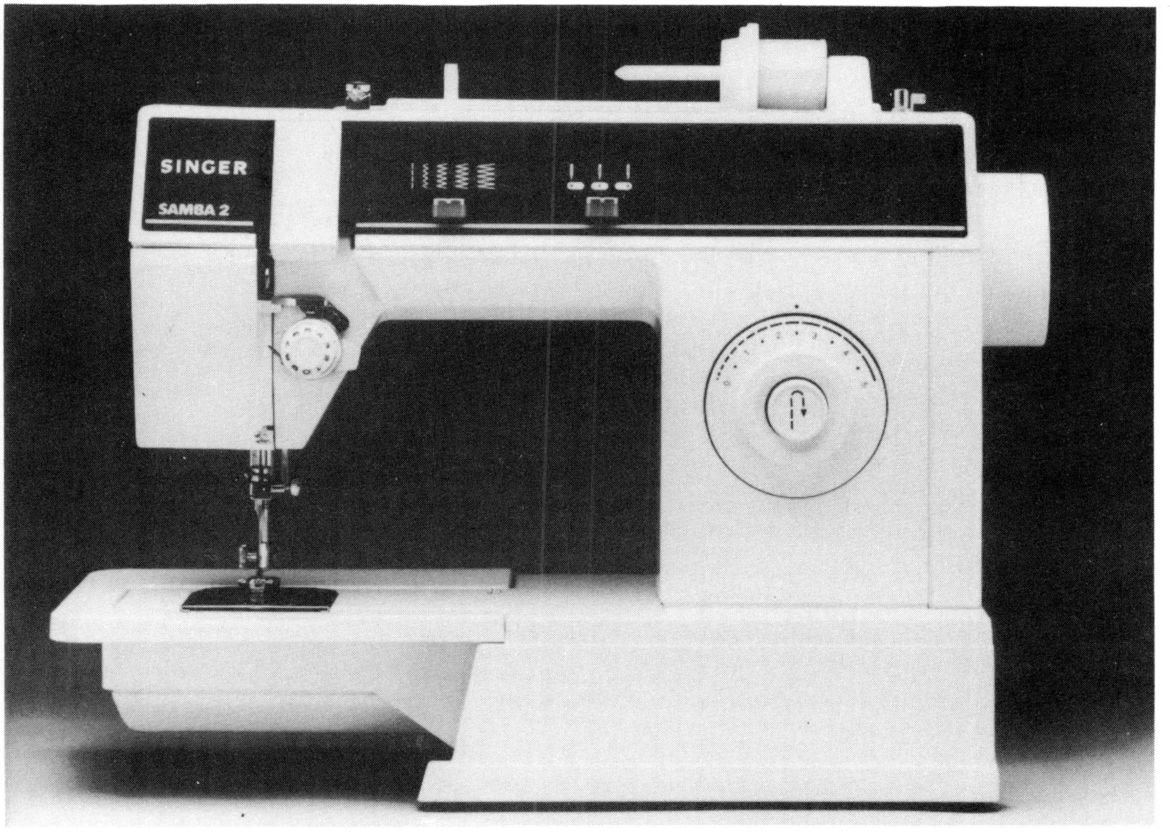

fig. 16. The Singer Samba 2. *An easy-to-use, no nonsense sewing machine with straight stitch and zig-zag, ideal for beginners. Photograph by courtesy of Singer Consumer Product Division*

a second-hand one so that when you do buy a better one you will be able to choose sensibly, knowing that you are competent enough to use its facilities.

Although there are occasional bargains, as a beginner you are unlikely to recognise them. Remember that, on the whole, you get what you pay for. If you buy an expensive machine made by one of the world's leading manufacturers it will be well-designed precision-made, properly tested and backed up with spare parts and service. It will also be easy to thread, easy to operate, it will be quiet, it won't go wrong, you will feel utterly confident and it will be a joy to touch and use. If you buy a cheap machine it will probably not be very quiet, it may be heavy and it will be limited in its functions. This does not mean you should not buy it, but you must not resent its limitations later.

Some cheap machines do not perform very well and some second-hand machines do not stitch well consistently. Check the following yourself by sitting at the machine, in the shop, with some pieces of your own material. Try and take a few pieces of fabric of different types, including at least one slippery polyester. See if the machine will:

Stop fairly quickly and not run on for more than a couple of stitches.

Sew properly through at least three layers of tough material such as denim.

Produce a stitch that looks the same on both sides of a double layer of fabric.

Maintain an even stitch length on a long line of stitching.

Keep two layers of fabric together reasonably; the upper layer not creeping forward.

Wind the bobbin evenly; uneven winding can result in uneven stitching.

Stitch in a straight line while you just lightly guide the fabric. Try this on the slippery fabric, the stitching should not vere away to one side.

Reverse easily and in a straight line.

Stitch a fairly wide zig-zag over a single edge of fabric as if neatening a seam, without the thread breaking.

Go slowly enough for you: as a beginner you will want a machine with two speeds.

Finally, don't go alone, take your competent friend with you and ask her to use all the machines before you make a decision.

If things go wrong

If your machine suddenly does not sew properly it is likely to be something very simple and not a major failure. Remember that most faults such as uneven stitching, missed stitches etc., are due to the needle being bent, blunt or the wrong size for the fabric, or to wrong threading. Always begin by re-threading the machine and if that does not cure it, put in a new, smaller size needle.

HOW TO SEW BY MACHINE

One thing I cannot help you with is the control and understanding of your machine.

It can be compared with learning to drive a car – you must use it as often as possible until the basic operations like threading, putting in fabric and taking it out, turning corners, are so familiar that you can perform them confidently without referring to the instruction book.

The following tips will help, but you must learn where the appropriate controls are. Begin by machining on lined or squared paper. Do not thread the machine but use all the controls, altering the stitch size etc., and sew straight lines, curves and corners until the perforations in the paper are accurate.

Only after practising should you thread the machine and sew on fabric. After threading sew a short line on a piece of fabric folded double. This is to make sure that the stitch looks a reasonable size for the fabric and also to ensure that the machine has been threaded correctly.

ITEMS NEEDED FOR MACHINING

Keep a few things in a drawer of the machine table, or in a box nearby so that they are to hand whenever you use the machine. Include the following:

Tailors' chalk
The additional feet and other machine accessories
Spare bobbins
Small scissors or a pair of thread snips for cutting thread ends neatly at the end of each line of stitching (fig. 17).
Pin box or a magnet to catch pins, or even a little dish for pins.
Brush for removing dust and fibres from the outside of the machine, round the needle area and inside the spool or bobbin sockets. A small decorator's paint brush is easiest to use. Get into the habit of using it each time you thread the machine or rewind a spool.

fig. 17

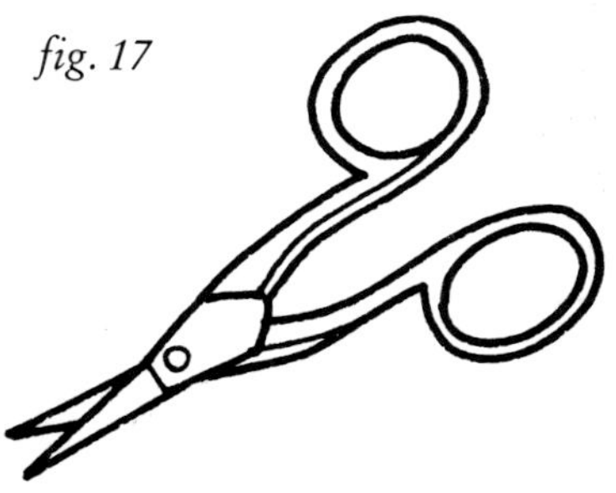

MACHINING TECHNIQUES

How to start

Begin by making sure that the needle is at its highest point: most modern models stop automatically with the needle in that position.

Slide the fabric under the foot from the front ensuring that the edge of the fabric is level with the back of the foot or even further back.

Lower the presser foot and stitch.

How to stop
Begin to ease your foot off the pedal about 3cm before the point where you want the needle to stop and then proceed slowly. Stop exactly in position by putting your hand on the balance wheel.

How to fasten off
Go into reverse for about three stitches and then cut.

How to turn corners
Stop, put needle down into fabric, lift presser foot, turn fabric, lower foot, stitch.

How to sew long lines of stitching
Sew in bursts of 5-6cm, stopping to reposition the fabric.

How to guide fabric
Place the fingers of both hands lightly on the fabric, do not push or pull.

Learn how to do blind hemming, gathering, and machine basting and also practise stitching accurately along a folded edge of fabric.

HOW TO MACHINE STRAIGHT

Make it easy for yourself by having guide lines for keeping machining straight. Here are some suggestions.

Make a row of dots on the fabric using a fabric marking pen.

Use tailor's chalk and a ruler to mark a line.

Use the edge of the machine foot as a guide by running the edge on the fabric edge.

Use one of the grooved lines on the machine bed as a guide for the edge of the fabric.

Cut a piece of basting tape and stick it down across the machine bed the distance you require from the needle.

The best guide of all is a well-pressed folded edge of fabric. By watching the needle carefully you can feed in a pressed edge and machine exactly on that edge for neat accurate top stitching.

YOUR SEWING MACHINE – CHECK LIST FOR TROUBLE SPOTS

Thread breakage

1. Improper threading of either top or bobbin thread
2. Starting machining with needle incorrectly positioned
3. Rough spots on needle eye, throat plate or bobbin case
4. Lint or thread ends around bobbin case
5. Needle too fine for fabric or thread
6. Needle improperly set
7. Bent needle
8. Tension too tight
9. Top thread caught around spool holder

Needle breakage

1. Wrong needle for machine
2. Presser foot improperly set
3. Stitching over pins, zip etc
4. Bobbin inserted incorrectly
5. Needle improperly set
6. Wrong size needle for fabric
7. Pulling fabric

7

SEWING BY HAND

Sewing by hand is slow but many beginners prefer it to machining for that reason and because it can be controlled.

The quilted waistcoat on page 71 can be made entirely by hand if you wish and by the time it is finished you will have had plenty of good practice at several stitches and techniques.

The skill of hand-sewing is one which has to be learnt and then practised in order to achieve small, neat, even stitches. When you reach that stage you will then be enjoying it and you will feel confident about the results.

With any craft you need instruction on how to use equipment properly. The following describes the correct sequence of hand sewing with reasons for doing it this way.

First collect together all your hand-sewing tools. Collect together all the parts of the garment requiring hand-sewing. Plan to have one session and hope that it will be uninterrupted. Press the fabric if necessary. Sit down comfortably.

fig. 18

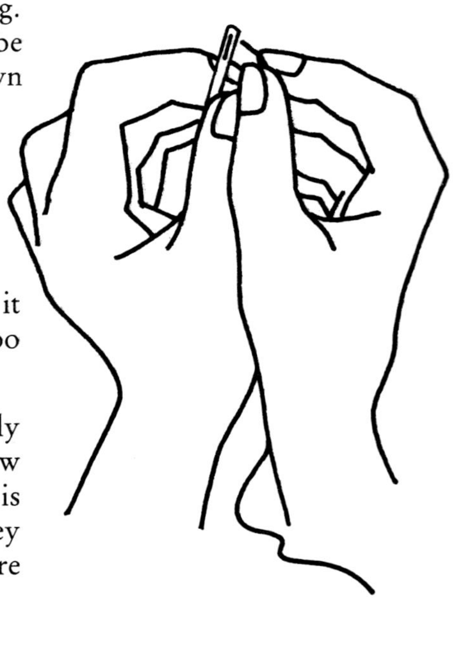

THREADING A NEEDLE (fig. 18)

Always thread a needle in the same way so that in time it becomes automatic and not something you have to think too much about.

1. Pull the thread from the reel to what will be a fairly precise length by moving your hand but keeping your elbow close to your body. This gives you a length of thread that is not too long to control. Long threads tend to tangle and they can wear before being used up. Long pieces of thread are slower and more laborious to use.

2. It is best to cut Drima by snipping it at an angle but Duet and tacking thread are best broken or bitten off.
3. Moisten the end and pass it through the eye of the needle. Rest both hands together while doing this to steady both the needle and the thread and as a beginner it helps to rest your elbows on the table.
4. Pull the end through the eye and draw it out so that it becomes the longer end and knot it.

HOW TO MAKE A KNOT (fig. 19)

As you draw the thread through the needle wind the end once round your forefinger, push the loop of thread off the end of the finger with your thumb. Pull the knot gently to the end of the thread between your thumb and forefinger. Learn to make knots this way, it is quick and the knots are the right size. Smaller knots will not be adequate, longer ones will look ugly and produce humps in the garment.

If at first you can't make a knot, try making sure the thread twists more times as you slide your thumb along your forefinger. Always put a knot in the end of the thread. There will nearly always be a convenient edge of fabric to conceal it under. If not, begin by making two backstitches then cut off the knot for neatness.

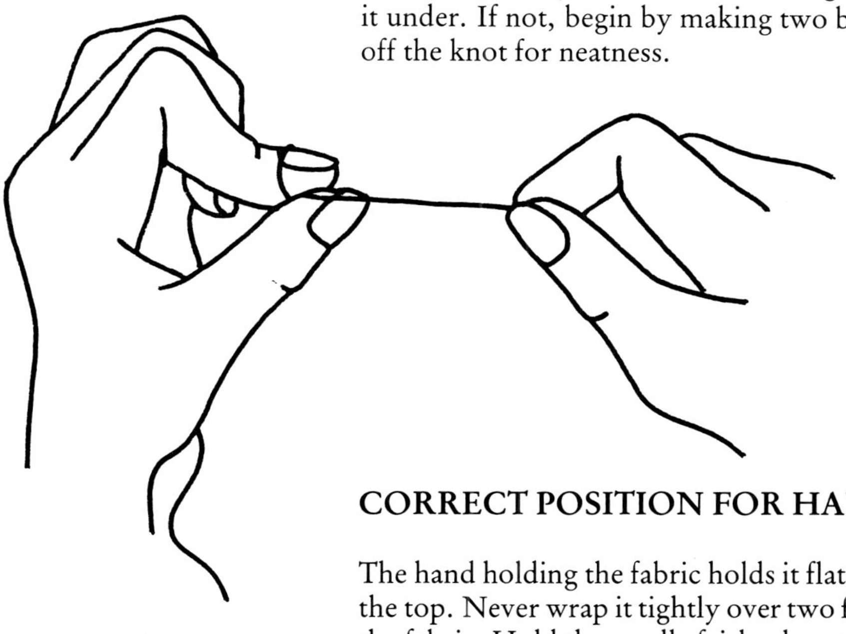

fig. 19

CORRECT POSITION FOR HANDS

The hand holding the fabric holds it flat with the thumbs on the top. Never wrap it tightly over two fingers as it stretches the fabric. Hold the needle fairly close to the point between thumb and forefinger in the other hand.

Keep the middle finger, with thimble on, close beside the forefinger so that the side of the thimble rests on the end of the needle. Holding the needle like this, insert it in and out of the fabric, using the thumb of the other hand to slightly push the fabric towards the point. Move thumb and forefinger from the needle and forward to take hold of the point, but the thimble still rests against the end so that it can push on the needle. Pull the needle and thread through and insert again.

Although this is a long explanation, once you have followed it a few times your stitches will be made quickly in a continuous flowing movement which will result in a neat even appearance.

HOW TO STITCH

Sit comfortably for all permanent stitching, hold the fabric up but support it at the right height on the table. Keep your head and shoulders still, moving your arm between hand and elbow only and moving it out to the side, not across the body. When the thread comes to an end, make two or three back stitches and cut off the end of thread. Re-thread the needle in the same way and start again.

TENSION

Even-sized stitches are the result of making smooth rather than jerky movements and of holding the needle correctly using the right length of thread, therefore putting the same tension on it each time it is pulled through the fabric. You will generally have a guide line to keep straight by, an edge of fabric, a crease or, when attaching bindings, a row of stitches.

Press hand stitching when finished using the toe of the iron.

USEFUL SEWING AIDS

A good haberdashery department will display a wide variety of sewing aids but you will not need them all. After providing yourself with the essential tools and equipment begin to look at some of the other things that are available. The following is a list of items that you may find useful.

Tracing wheel (fig. 20)
A small wheel with a handle, used for marking and copying paper patterns. The spikes on the wheel perforate the paper and it can also be used for marking fabric. Fold a piece of dressmakers' carbon paper, slide it between two layers of fabric, run the wheel over the pattern markings on the top of the fabric and a coloured line appears on one side of each layer. The spiked wheel makes a dotted line, a clearer continuous line is made by using a smooth tracing wheel.

fig. 20

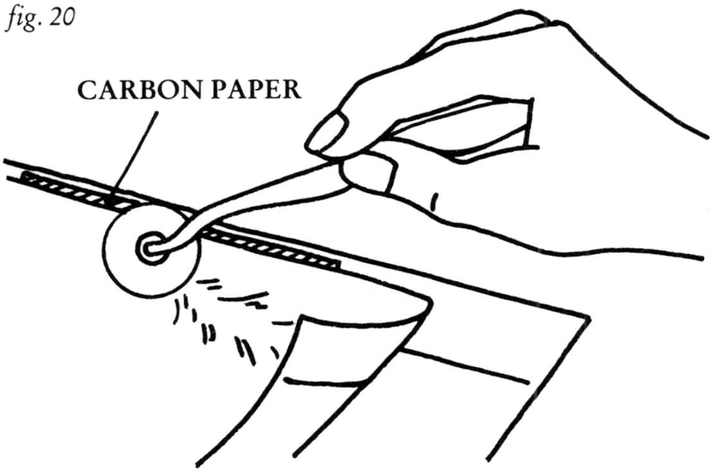

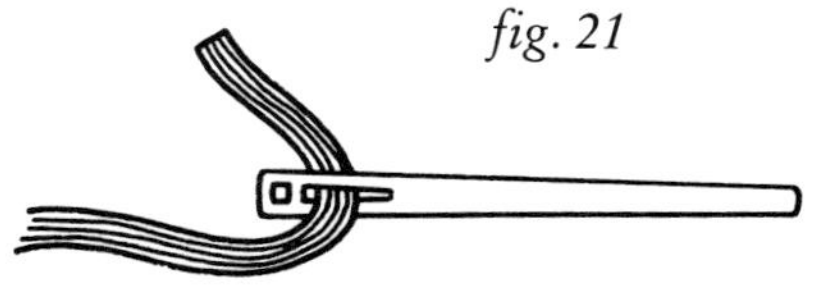

fig. 21

Elastic threader (fig. 21)
A short flat metal needle with a large eye. It is best to sew the elastic to the end of the eye rather than tie it.

fig. 22

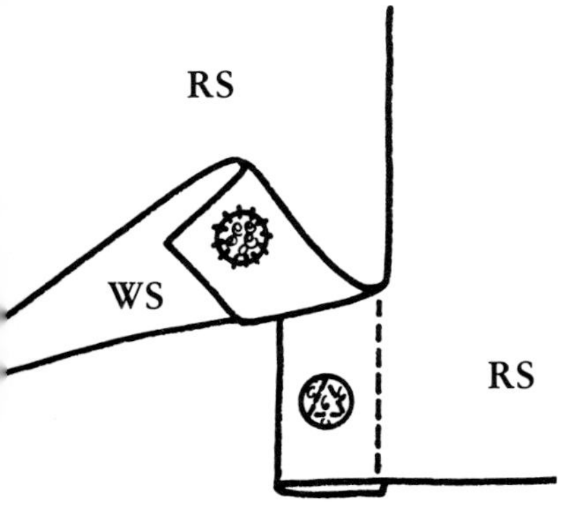

Velcro (fig. 22)
Velcro can be used as a fastening in lots of places. On waist-bands or other places where there will be strain in wear be sure to use a piece at least 4cm long; elsewhere, such as cuffs, it can be as short as 1.5cm. Circles of Velcro, called 'Spot-Ons' can be used in place of buttonholes and buttons and in place of press studs and hooks. Attach Velcro with a small machine zig-zag stitch or with hemming stitch by hand if you wish the stitching to be less obvious. Spot-Ons can be hemmed all round or attached with a triangle of machine stitching across each circle.

Petersham and belt backing

These can both be used in belts and petersham can also be used instead of a waistband round the top of a skirt or trousers. Curved petersham provides a comfortable fit but it cannot be fastened as tightly round the waist as straight petersham.

Bias binding

Most bias binding is in plain-coloured cotton or polyester cotton fabric, a few are printed designs and satin binding is also available. Binding is folded ready to use and is therefore quicker than making your own. It is bought pre-packed on cards; some is available by the metre.

Trims

These are button sets that you cover with your own fabric. They are easy to use and are available in several sizes.

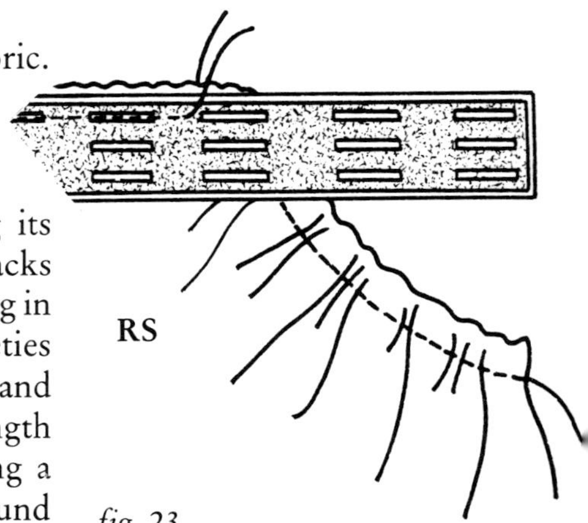

fig. 23

Fold-a-band (fig. 23)

This is interfacing in a strip with perforations along its length for easy, accurate folding. It is available in pre-packs or by the metre. Lightweight Fold-a-Band is for inserting in cuffs, straps, fastenings, pocket tops. The heavier varieties are made in two widths, have three rows of perforations and are for waistbands. To use Fold-a-Band, cut the length required, press it to the wrong side of the fabric using a medium-hot iron and a damp pressing cloth, cut out round the outside. A seam allowance has to be added to the lightweight variety when cutting out. Attach to the garment using the edge and perforations as guides.

Wundaweb (fig. 24)

A product that can be used in place of stitching to hold up hems on some fabrics. It is sold in packs containing 4m of a fine non-woven web 2.5cm wide. To use, place it between two layers of fabric, making sure it is completely covered, arrange the fabric and Wundaweb so that both are flat and press using a hot iron and a damp cloth. It is necessary to press several times in each spot in order to ensure that the heat and moisture penetrate that fabric and thoroughly melt the Wundaweb. Use on hems in medium-weight firm fabrics; try it out first on light fabrics.

Wundaweb is also very useful in other areas, for example

fig. 24

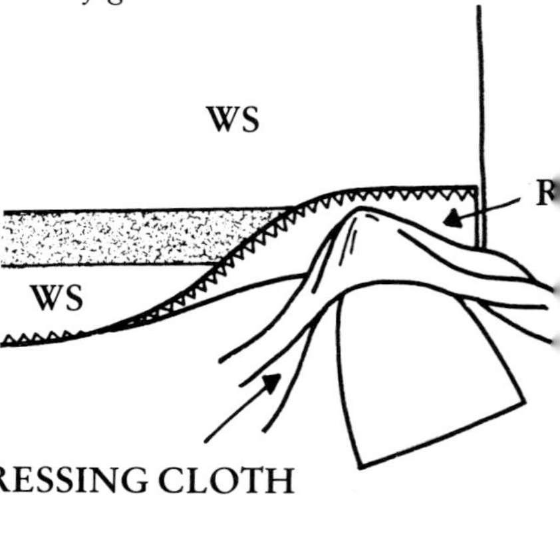

small pieces placed underneath a facing will hold it in position and eliminate the need for stitching. There is also a specially strong Wundaweb for use on denim hems.

Hooks and eyes and press studs (fig. 25)

fig. 25

These are all fiddly to sew but sometimes there is no easy alternative to using them. It is best if there are two layers of material and the strongest, neatest way of attaching them is with buttonhole stitch. It is worth learning how to do this in order to ensure that hooks and press studs don't come loose in wear. Press studs fasten one layer of garment on top of another and hold them together. Hooks and eyes can fasten layers or they can be used for edge to edge fastenings. The fastening withstands more strain but it can be slightly wobbly. Using a bar instead of an eye is firmer. The finer the fabric the smaller should be the hook or press stud you use.

Mark the position you wish to place them using a fabric pen.

fig. 26

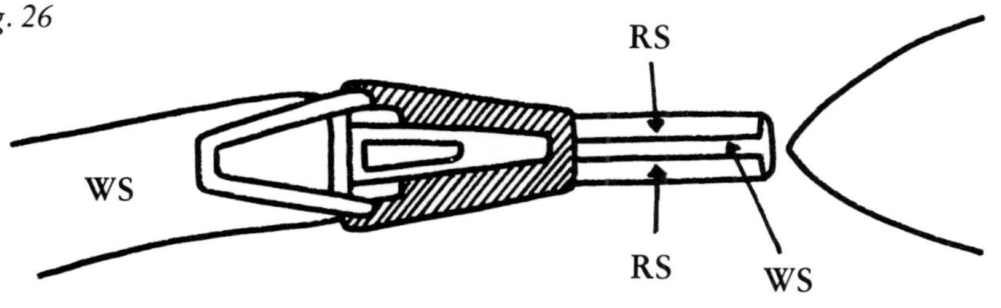

Bias binding tool or tape marker (fig. 26)

A useful tool if you want to make bias binding from your own fabric. Cut crossway strips in fabric the width stated on the instructions. Pass the fabric through it and press it as it emerges and it is ready for use. The tool is available in two sizes. It is best to use the 12mm size to bind the waistcoat on page 71.

Dressmakers' carbon paper

This is sold in packets containing several sheets in various colours. It is easy to use if you cut the sheets into strips 8cm wide, fold them lengthwise with the shiny side out and, having cut out your fabric right side out, slide the carbon paper between the layers of fabric with the pattern on top. Use a tracing wheel to run along the seam lines or darts and move the paper as necessary.

Beware of using strong colours on white or pale fabric as it does not always wash out. Never use carbon paper on the right side of any fabric.

ITEMS NEEDED FOR HAND-SEWING

Needles
There are various types for things such as embroidery but for straightforward sewing buy a couple of packets in assorted sizes from 5 or 6 (large) up to 7 or 8 (small). The finer your fabric the smaller the needle you should use. Consult the chart on page 20 for guidance.

TYPES
Betweens or Egg-Eyed Betweens are dressmakers' needles. They are short, comfortable to use and it is easy to produce small neat stitches because you can hold the needle in the correct position. Sharps are longer and are also for general sewing.

Small scissors
You must have a small pair of good quality scissors with very sharp points. They are for trimming threads and snipping seams. Buy a pair with large finger holes as they are comfortable to use. Those with short blades are accurate and easy to control as the tips are not too far from your hand. Hold small scissors with the thumb in the upper grip, your second finger in the lower one and use your forefinger to support and control the shaft of the scissors.

Thimble (fig. 27)
A thimble is a help only if it is used correctly; when you are experienced you will find that you cannot sew without one. Wear it on the middle finger so that its side rests against the end of the needle as you take a stitch. If you find closed-top thimbles clumsy or uncomfortable, try the one the professionals use, the sort with an open top.

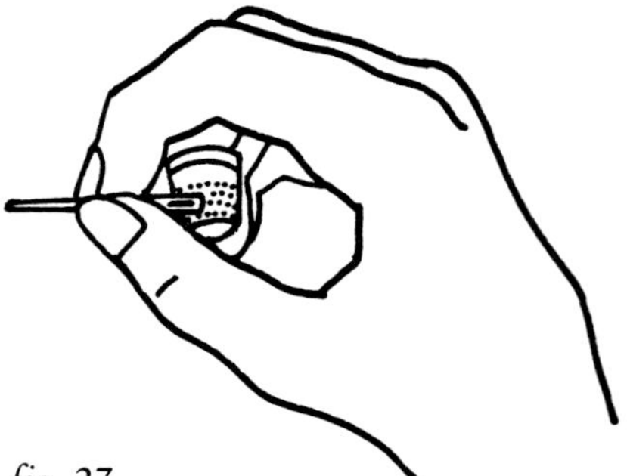

fig. 27

Sewing and cutting board
This is a large board that unfolds to 190cm x 100cm and which you put either over your dining table or on the bed or floor.

Spread out your fabric on it to cut out. The board has on it a printed grid of 2.5cm squares. Use the lines to ensure that fabric is laid out straight then mark out or pin your pattern to the fabric. The board will also have some diagonal lines to use as a guide when cutting bias strips of fabric to use as binding.

Keep your sewing on the board for tacking and similar jobs. When you sit down in a chair to do hand sewing fold up the board and have it across your lap to support the fabric and provide a sewing surface.

Use the grid to scale up diagram patterns such as those in this book. To do this place a large sheet of tracing paper or plain pattern paper over the board and transfer the outline of the pattern using the grid lines to guide you. Some diagram patterns are outlined on a grid in small scale and it is very easy to scale them up using a board, by counting the squares.

To make a durable pattern that can be used several times use light Sew-in Vilene interfacing instead of using paper.

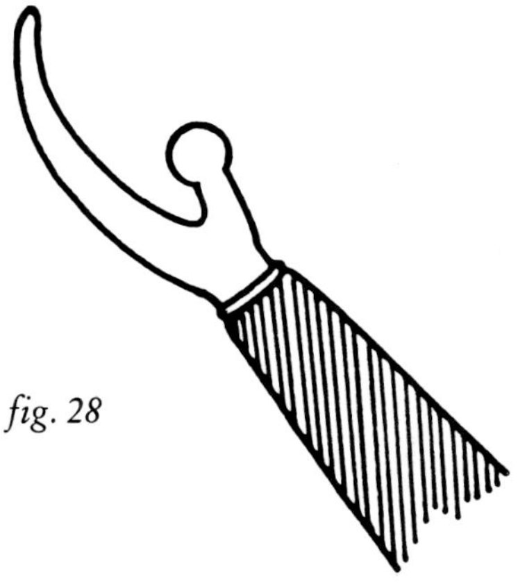

fig. 28

Unpicker (fig. 28)
It is a mistake to start sewing thinking you might soon be unpicking but this is a useful tool. It is also called a seam ripper. The point can be used for removing stitches. The blade can be used for cutting machine-made buttonholes, but it must be handled with care. Stop it from slipping too far by putting a pin in the fabric in front of the blade.

fig. 29

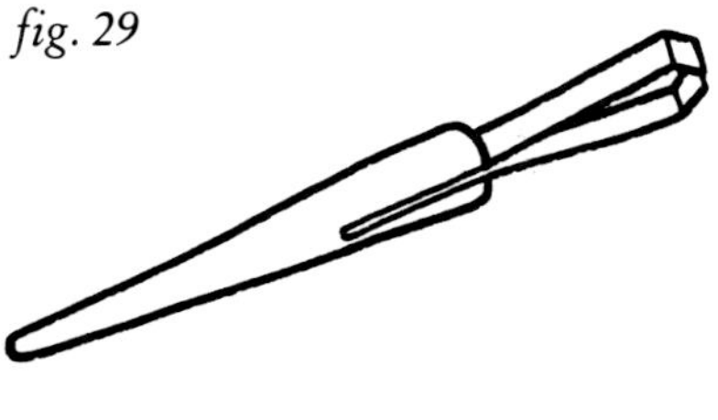

Bodkin (fig. 29)
Not essential but very useful this is a bone or plastic tool used for removing tacking stitches more safely than with scissor points. Use it too for pushing into corners of collars or belts to shape them. A modern bodkin also has useful tweezers set into the end of the handle.

Rouleau needle (fig. 30)
It is well worth buying one of these. It is an extremely useful tool that is used for turning narrow tubing after stitching. Slip the ball-end of the needle into the end of the tube and sew the eye of the needle to the fabric. Ease the tubing onto the needle until the ball appears then pull the needle to turn the tube of fabric right side out. Cut off the needle and trim the ends of the tube.

The needle can also be used for turning ties or belts right

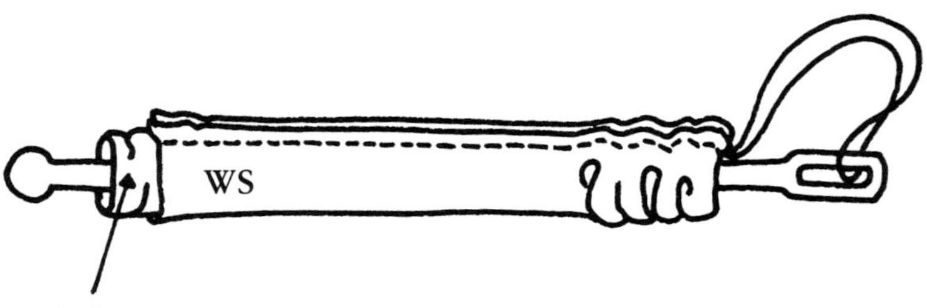

fig. 30

side out simply by pushing the ball-end against the fabric, and use it also for threading elastic.

Beeswax (fig. 31)
An essential little item that is inexpensive and invaluable. One cake will last for years. When sewing on buttons use the thread doubled through the needle then run it over the beeswax a couple of times and twist it for strength. When using sewing thread doubled the two threads will part easily making it difficult to make neat stitches. Correct this by running it lightly over the beeswax.

Beeswax can be used for a variety of other things too including easing zip teeth that stick.

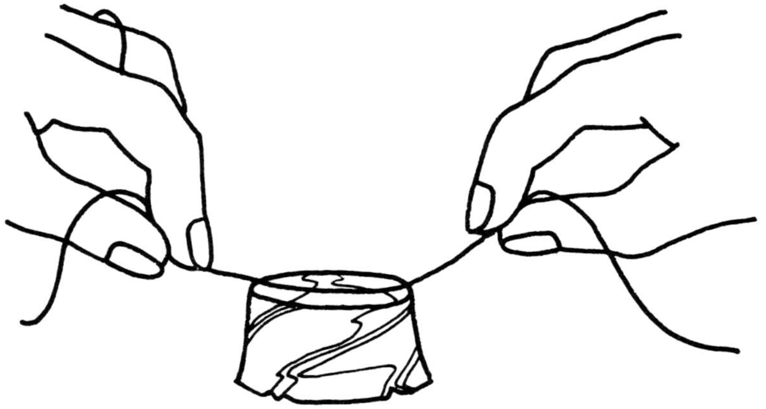

fig. 31

8

HAND-SEWING STITCHES

As this is the most traditional area of sewing and subject to so little change there are very few stitches that you need to learn in order to do hand-sewing. As you become more experienced you will find instructions in more advanced books on variations for specific purposes but until then you need only master the following.

TACKING (fig. 32)

An easy stitch because it can be quite large and as it is removed later in the process you need not worry about making it perfectly neat. However, it is worth learning the correct technique for making even-sized stitches because it makes it quicker to do and holds the fabric more effectively. Use tacking to hold layers of fabric together temporarily. Use a needle a size larger than for the small permanent stitching on the garment and use tacking thread.

Begin by arranging the fabric flat on the table if possible. Pull a length of tacking thread from the reel; get used to pulling it to the length of your arm when extended so that each piece you use will be of similar length and you will become accustomed to controlling it. Break the thread at the reel, it is quicker than stopping to pick up scissors. Moisten the broken end and thread the needle, pulling it through and making a knot in the same end.

Make stitches by inserting the needle in the fabric until you feel the table beneath, use the fingers of your other hand to gently move the fabric a little so that it forms a bump at the needle. You can then lift the point of the needle out of the fabric. The amount of fabric you pick up should be as little as possible, as little as 5mm if you can manage it. Work

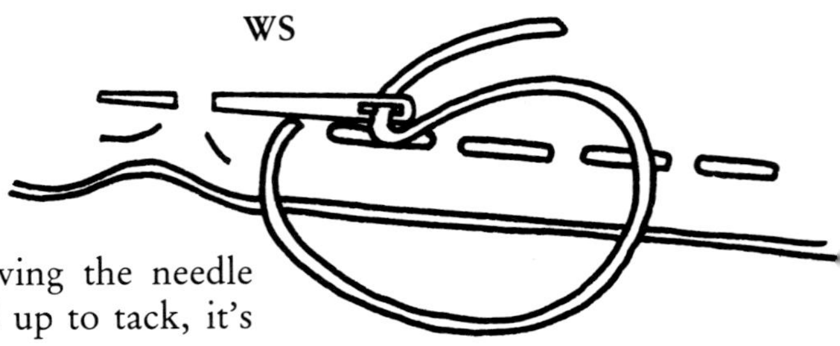

fig. 32

from right to left across your body moving the needle forward 2 or 3cm between stitches. Stand up to tack, it's quicker and less tiring.

If the shape of the fabric is such that you cannot keep it on the table, sit down and hold it comfortably in front of you. You should be able to make slightly smaller stitches if you tack this way.

When you reach the end of the process or the end of the thread fasten off by making one extra stitch over the last one.

After stitching the fabric permanently pull the knot of the tacking to remove most of it then ease out the rest. Tacking stitches will come out easily if you use proper tacking thread, which is soft, and if you end with only one back stitch.

Remember to re-use your longer lengths of tacking thread.

RUNNING STITCH

This is a small, even hand-stitch used for gathering. Use a long piece of sewing thread with a knot in the end and a No. 7 needle. Work on the right side of the fabric, hold the needle so that you move the point in and out making several stitches before pulling the needle through. You may find it easier to control it when you pull up the gathers if you insert two rows of running stitches 3mm apart.

If you have long rows of gathering to do it is quicker to do it by machine; *see information on p. 55.*

BACK STITCH (fig. 33)

A hand-stitch that looks like machine-stitching. Use it only on the inside as it is not particularly neat. Use a No. 7 or 8

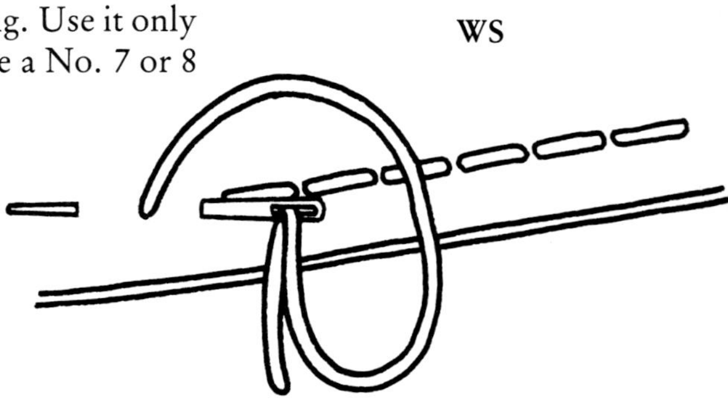

fig. 33

needle and a short piece of Drima, start with a knot hidden under an edge of fabric and make each stitch by taking the point of the needle half way back to the previous stitch. Pass the needle through the fabric, underneath and out again in one movement. For an equivalent stitch to use on the outside of a garment *see* Prick stitch.

HEMMING STITCH (fig. 34)

This hand-stitch is not really used on garment hems because it can be seen on the right side, but it is useful where a small, strong stitch is needed and where there is a fold of fabric on top of another layer. Use a size No. 7 or 8 needle and a short piece of Drima. Put a knot in the end and conceal it under the fold when you take the first stitch. Insert the needle in the fabric and then in the fold.

fig. 34

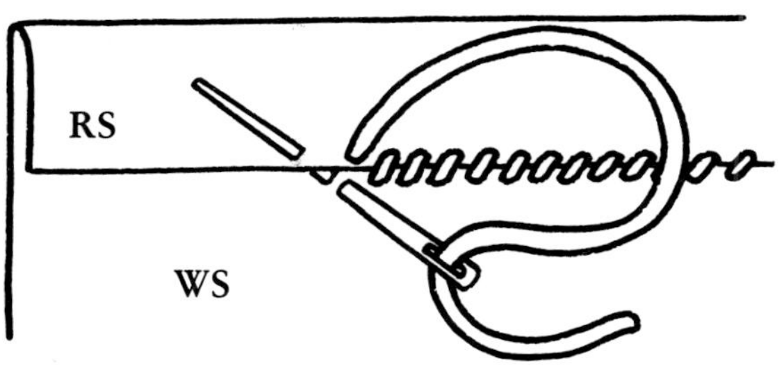

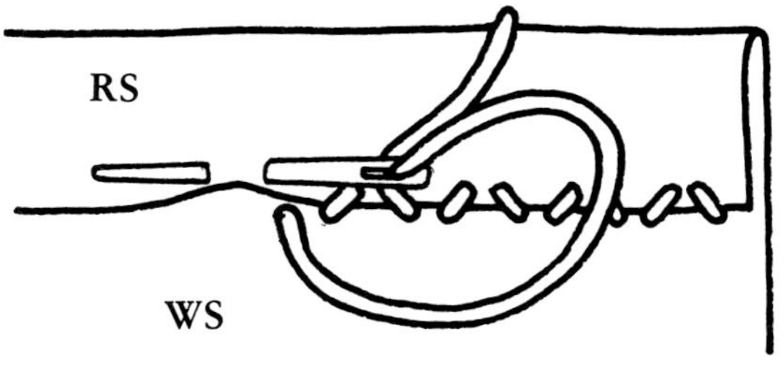

fig. 35

SLIP HEMMING (fig. 35)

This is the stitch to use on hems of skirts for example, where the fabric has been turned up twice and you therefore have a fold to stitch into. Use short lengths of thread, knot the end and tuck the knot under the fold. Pick up one or two threads or yarns of fabric on the needle close to the fold. Without pulling the needle through move the point immediately into the fold of the fabric and slide it along for about 5mm. Bring out the point of the needle and pull the thread through. Pick up another small amount of fabric, slide the needle along the fold, and so on. Do not pull the stitches tight or the hemline will show on the outside of the garment. Fasten off the thread with two back stitches in the fold.

OVERSEWING STITCH (fig. 36)

This is a small, neat stitch that is used for joining two folded edges of fabric on the right side. It is strong and stitches should be made as small as possible so that they are not too consipicuous. Use a short piece of thread, start with a knot concealed under one edge and work from right to left inserting the needle at right angles to the edges of the fabric.

fig. 36

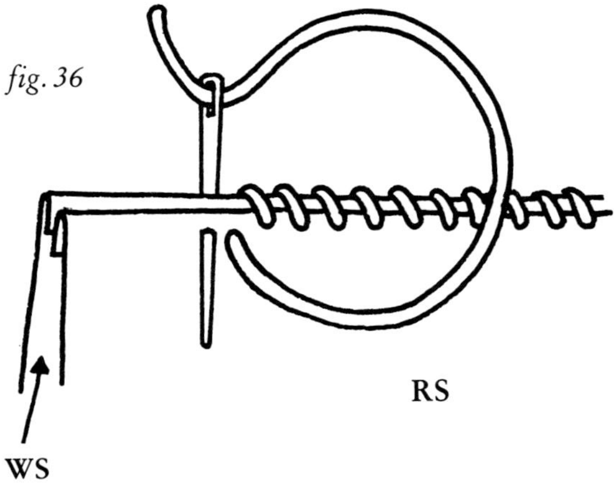

fig. 37

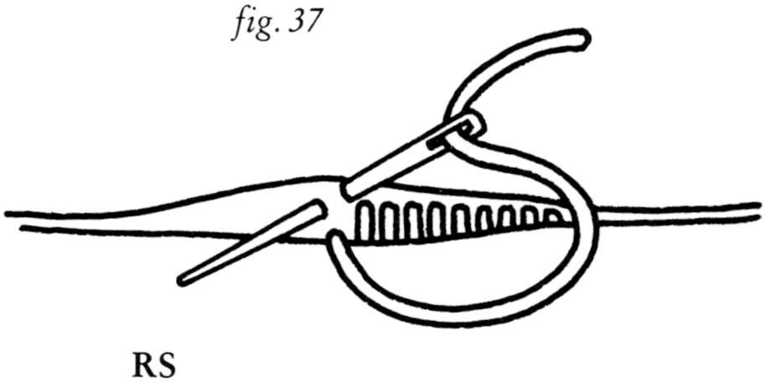

SLIP STITCH (fig. 37)

This stitch has a similar function to oversewing stitch but it can be completely concealed. It will not withstand much strain. One example of its use is stitching up the gap in the edge of a tie belt after turning it right-side-out. Use a short piece of thread, start with a knot concealed between the folds of fabric and work from right to left, taking small stitches alternately along each fold of fabric.

LOOP STITCH (fig. 38)

A simple stitch with not many uses but it can often be used to tidy up several stitches that might otherwise spoil a good effect. It can also be used in the same places as oversewing but it would be more conspicuous. If you have a very short raw edge of fabric that requires neatening, loop stitch is the best hand stitch to use.

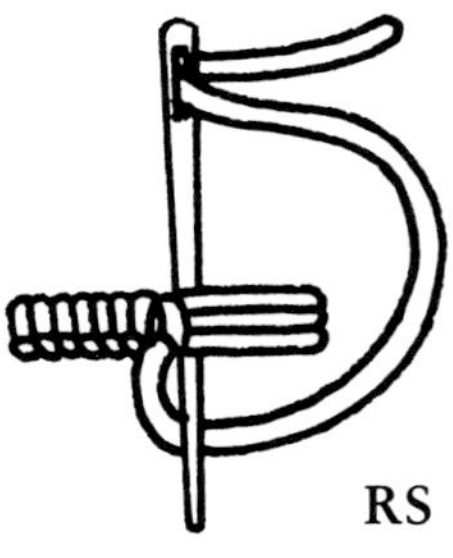

fig. 38

BAR TACK (fig. 38)

This is made of several short, straight stitches worked so closely that they are on top of each other. It is used to strengthen points that are likely to be strained in wear, for example the top of the side slit in the tunic on page 48.

To make a bar tack by hand insert three to four stitches 4mm in length, stabbing the needle through all layers of fabric, working with the fabric right side up. Use perfectly matching thread so that the bar will not be too obvious and finish it by working loop stitch over the threads. To do this bring the needle up at the left of the bar, slide the point under the stitches towards you and pull the thread through. Repeat until the bar is covered with small knots. Pass the needle to the wrong side and fasten off.

To make a bar tack by machine set the machine to a wide zig-zag and satin stitch and work four to six stitches. Cut off the thread ends. These bars can be made a little bigger and worked in contrast thread and used as decoration on a garment edge.

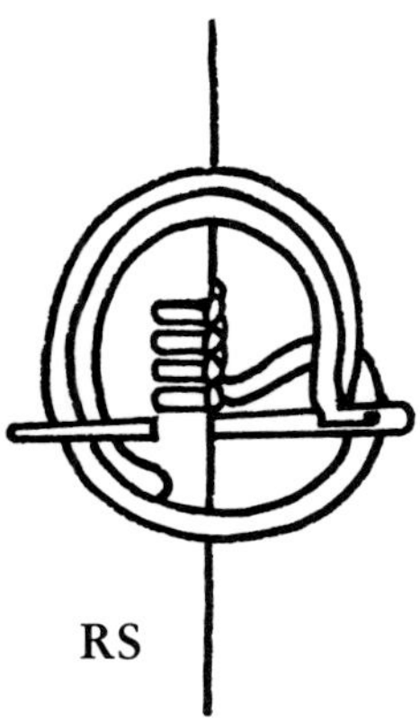

BUTTONHOLE STITCH (fig. 39)

fig. 39

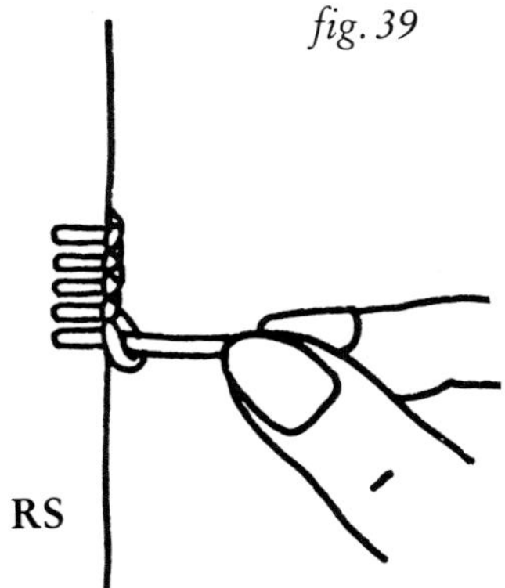

Leave this stitch until you feel you are becoming familiar with hand-sewing. Buttonhole stitches must be neat and even-sized and all the knots made with the same amount of tension on the thread. It is the stitch used for hand-worked buttonholes but you will not be attempting those until you are quite expert at sewing. Instead, use it to sew on hooks and eyes; it can also be used to attach Velcro and in places where a strong deep stitch is needed and where the tiny knots will look better than the bigger stitches.

Use a short piece of thread with a knot. Make a stitch in the fabric, take the part of the thread that is by the eye of the needle and wind it, holding both parts of it, round the point of the needle, and underneath it. Take hold of the point of the needle and pull it through slowly. When it is nearly through take hold of the thread close to the fabric, pull it gently and you will see a little knot form. Make all subsequent stitches very close to each other so that all the knots lie close together making a neat ridge. Try not to join new thread in the middle of a row of buttonhole stitches.

Fasten off by passing the needle to the wrong side of the fabric and work two back stitches.

PRICK STITCH (fig. 40)

A stitch worked by hand on the right side of fabric producing a row of stitches so small they appear as dents. It can be used in place of machine stitching for jobs like putting in zips, sewing in sleeves and for quilting. Use a No. 7 or 8 needle and short pieces of thread.

fig. 40

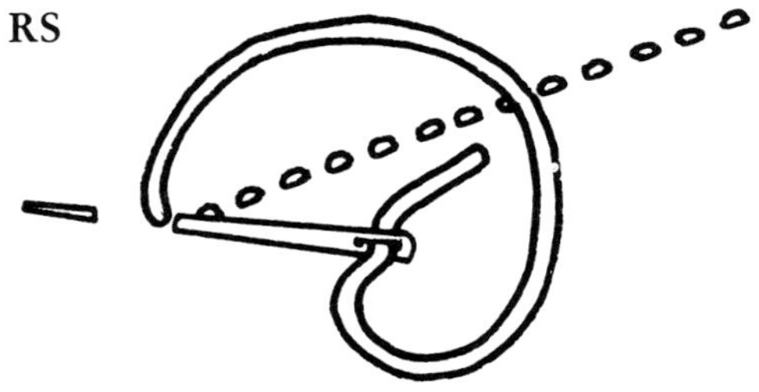

9

HOW TO PRESS

When you begin sewing there seems so much to learn about techniques and tools, as well as fabrics and stitches, that the necessity to use the iron seems irrelevant. But whatever else you ignore, omit, gloss over or forget, try from the start to stick to one golden rule which is to GET OUT THE IRON AND IRONING BOARD BEFORE ANYTHING when you plan to do some sewing. Pressing your sewing isn't something your teacher dreamed up as a penalty, it is in fact the thing that can improve your work almost beyond recognition. The iron is the most vital piece of sewing equipment you have. Even your first rows of wobbly, wrinkled machining, your first bit of hemming, will look perfectly all right, maybe even good, after you have pressed it.

Use the iron in two ways. Use it to keep your sewing fresh: try to hang your fabric and half-made garment on a hanger between sessions but if it does get creased don't work on it while it looks depressing, run the iron over it to freshen it and make it look new again.

Use it also on processes. Try to remember this: press before – press afterwards – press again. Whether you have turned up a hem, tacked down a binding, turned in an edge for a zip, or anything else you can name, press it before you stitch it. Then finish it off and press it again. You will then go on to complete other areas of the garment and finally you must press the whole thing again before you wear it.

When you use the iron on processes try to learn to manipulate it. Think of the toe of the iron as a very small shape that can be gently fitted into odd corners, that will smooth out stitching, that will give you a good crease on an edge or a hem. Hold the iron in place long enough for it to take effect.

Finally, start thinking of the iron as a weight to be 'plonked' to be effective. Try not to swish it about because you will get wrinkled fabric, in addition the process itself will not be properly pressed.

The iron

Use a steam iron if you have one. If it has been used for normal laundering for some time it would be worth having it overhauled to ensure steam can flow freely and evenly and to have a new sole plate fitted to ensure that fabric is not harmed.

Always use the iron with care, manipulating its toe into difficult areas.

IRON CLEANER

A cleaning stick made by Vilene, this is easy to use and will remove scorch marks and adhesive from interfacing from the sole plate of your iron. Follow the instructions for use on the package.

Pressing cloth

When you begin sewing you will find that a steam iron is adequate for pressing all the fabrics you use but if you later start to use heavier or more difficult cloth the only way to press it well is to place a dampened cloth over the fabric and place the iron on it. The effect is to put more steam into the fabric. A cloth is also very useful if you do not want to put the iron directly onto the fabric. This may be the case with embossed or pile fabrics or those with decoration such as beading or embroidery. In this case the cloth is used dry. You should use this method when pressing the quilted waistcoat on page 71, if you use a delicate fabric or if you add beads to the quilting.

The best fabric to use as a pressing cloth is butter-muslin. You will find it in household linen departments. Buy one metre. When you use it damp, wet it throughly then wring it out tightly to make sure there is no surplus water to drop onto the garment fabric. Use the iron sharply on the damp muslin, removing the iron and the cloth immediately.

Ironing board

Keep it accessible because you will need it each time you sew. Make sure the padding and the cover are smooth and unworn. If they are not, spend a little time stripping and recovering the board. The best padding consists of two layers of blanket or soft coating on top of one layer of foam. Cut them to fit the board with the edges only just over the edge of the board. Never have bunches of surplus fabric pinned under the board or you will be unable to slide your sewing over it.

Fix the covering with a staple gun or double-sided sticky tape. Make a cover to fit the board exactly, having the seam round the board but below the edge and fasten it with three or four pairs of tapes tied underneath. The best fabric to use is polyester and cotton sheeting – buy a pretty print in pale colours. Dispense with aluminium ironing board covers: they rarely fit the board, are noisy and harsh to use, and they do not produce the best finish on your pressing.

Sleeve board and pads

When you have made a few things it would be worth buying a sleeve board or even a new ironing board with its own sleeve board. The sleeve board provides a narrow padded area onto which you can slide waists, trouser hems, cuffs, necklines and other small processes. The sleeve board is raised above the ironing board which is a better height for pressing, the remainder of the garment then rests on the main board and does not pull on the part you are pressing.

Pressing pads can be bought in various shapes and you will only find these useful if you get to the stage where you do a lot of sewing.

10

SOME EASY-TO-MAKE DESIGNS

All the advice in this book about choosing fabrics and paper patterns applies to anything you may wish to make but to help you make a quicker and slightly cheaper start on your sewing the following pages give you some simple things to make by following a diagram instead of a paper pattern.

You must have the items of equipment given on the basic list and you must have equipment for pressing. Apart from that all you need are the fabric and items of haberdashery given for each article.

When you have made these things and wish to progress to paper patterns read the section of the book on page 79 entitled Commercial Paper Patterns.

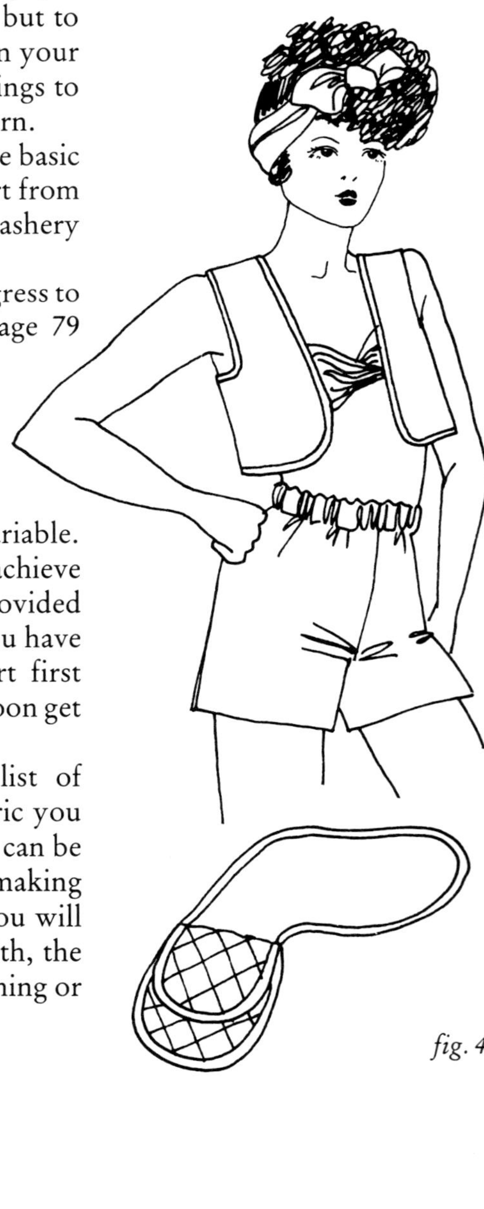

fig. 41

WHAT TO MAKE FIRST

All the garments are very simple but stylish and variable. They also team up well with each other. You will achieve good results, however little experience you have, provided you follow the instructions and hints carefully. If you have never done any sewing you should make the skirt first because it is the quickest pattern to cut out and you soon get on to the sewing.

Before you go and buy the fabric read the list of suggestions and also make a note of how much fabric you need to buy. To keep it very simple all the garments can be cut from fabric that is 115cm wide so when you are making your selection look only at fabrics of that width. You will find a swing ticket or label on the roll giving the width, the fibre content and, possibly, instructions for dry cleaning or washing.

fig. 42

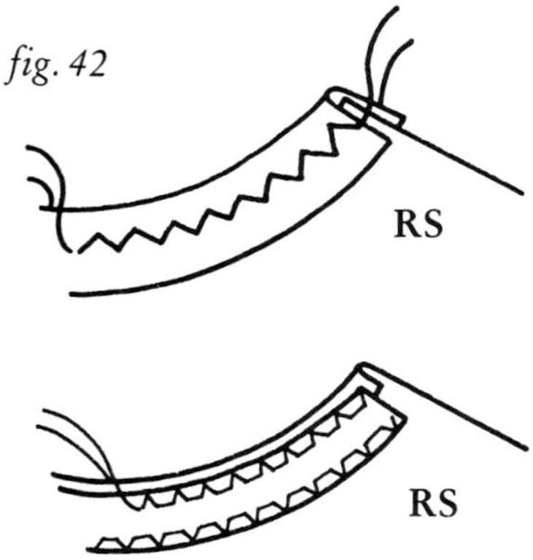

How to attach braid

You will need 70cm of folded braid for the neckline of the tunic. Select a braid with 'give' that will easily go round the curves. Either tack it in position or put a piece of basting tape in position on the garment, peel the backing off the tape and press the braid in position on top. Have the ends of braid meeting, turned in, at the shoulder of the tunic and hold the edges together by working oversewing stitch across the folds. Machine the braid to the tunic. On narrow flat braid sew a line of small zig-zag stitch down the middle; with wide or convex braid or cord, work a very small zig-zag or embroidery stitch down each edge; with very narrow

braid or ribbon, set the machine to a zig-zag stitch slightly wider than the braid and stitch right over it. Press the stitching lightly on completion.

THE TUNIC (pattern 1)

You will need 140cm of any soft or crisp cotton fabric 115cm wide and two reels of Drima or Duet.

1. Open out the fabric, slide it under the machine needle with the right side up and stitch round the neckline with zig-zag stitch to neaten the edge.

2. Arrange the neckline flat on the ironing board wrong side up and press the stitching. Fold over the edge about 1cm all round the neck and press. Fold and press a litttle at a time and place the toe of the iron on the fold of the fabric. On reaching the ends of the neckline you will find the edge will not lie flat so, using small scissors, snip through the zig-zag stitching in several places until you can fold over the edge and press it flat (fig. 43). If the edge springs up again either tack round the neckline by hand or hold the edge down with a few pieces of basting tape.

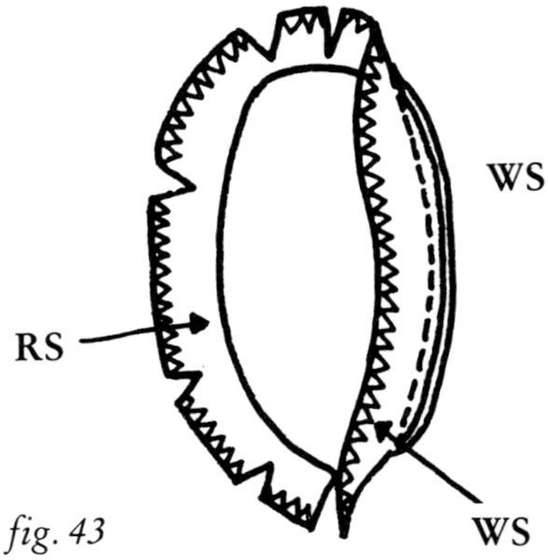

fig. 43

3. Turn the tunic right side up, slide it under the machine foot and stitch round the neckline. Select your stitch from the following:

A medium-length straight stitch worked very close to the edge and a second row a short distance away, use the edge of the foot as a guide.

A neat open machine embroidery stitch or even the blind stitch or other attractive utility stitch (fig. 44). One row of straight or small zig-zag stitch the width of the foot from the fold, to be covered with braid, cord, ric-rac braid or any similar decoration.

fig. 44
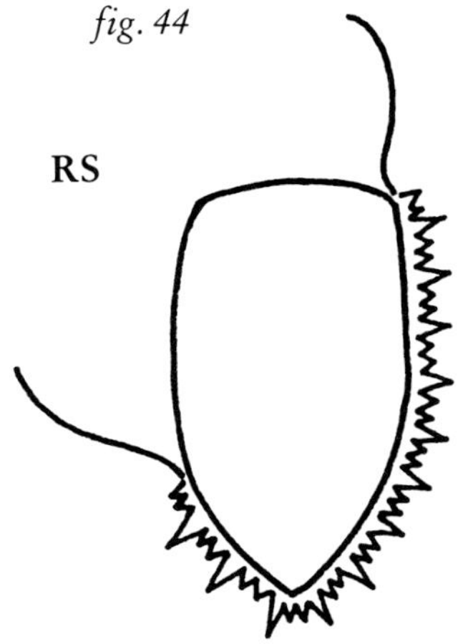

4. With tunic right side up work zig-zag stitch over the edge all round to neaten it. Press all stitching and the neckline.

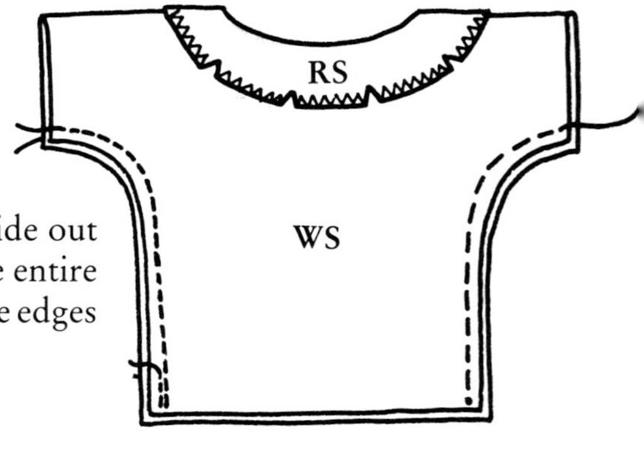

fig. 45

5. Fold the tunic at shoulders with fabric wrong side out until the edges meet at the sides and underarm. If the entire piece of fabric does not fit onto your table, prevent the edges

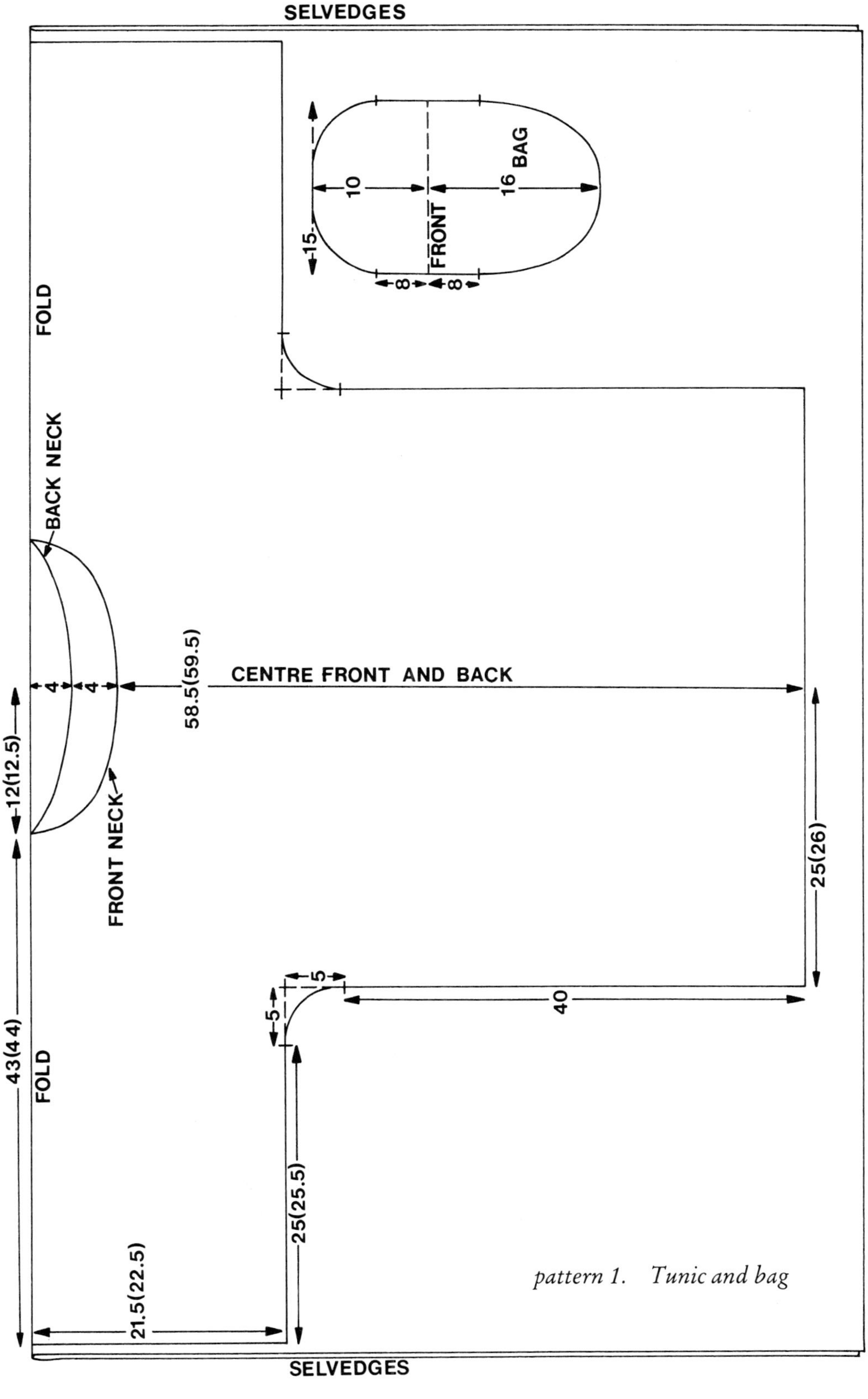

pattern 1. Tunic and bag

slipping apart by inserting three or four pins at intervals between the hemline and the sleeve edge.

Thread a No. 6 needle with tacking thread and tack along the seams from hem to sleeve edge. Try to stitch approximately 1.5cm inside the raw edge.

6. Put the tunic into the machine and stitch with a straight stitch from hem to sleeve edge using the groove on the machine to ensure that the stitching is 1.5cm from the edge. Fasten off the machining by reversing at the start and finish of each seam. Place tunic flat on the ironing board and press the stitching.

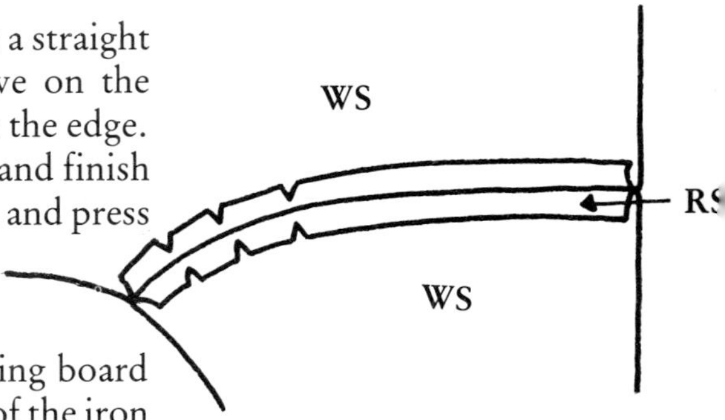

fig. 46

7. Open out the tunic and slide it onto the ironing board wrong side up with the seam straight. Use the toe of the iron and press open the side seams, then press firmly. At the underarm curve make three or four snips almost to the machine stitching, then press the seam open with the point of the iron. Turn the tunic right side out and press the seams again.

8. Turn the tunic wrong side out onto the ironing board and fold up the hem edge about 3cm press well. Turn up the sleeves by 3cm and press.

9. Secure the pressed hems, either by putting Wundaweb under the edge and pressing it until it is firmly stuck, or stitch by machine. To stitch by machine mark a guideline on the right side of the fabric using tailor's chalk, a chalk pencil or a fabric pen. Turn the tunic right side out, slide it onto the ironing board and rule a dotted line round the hem 2.5cm above the edge, and round the sleeve 2.5cm above the edge.

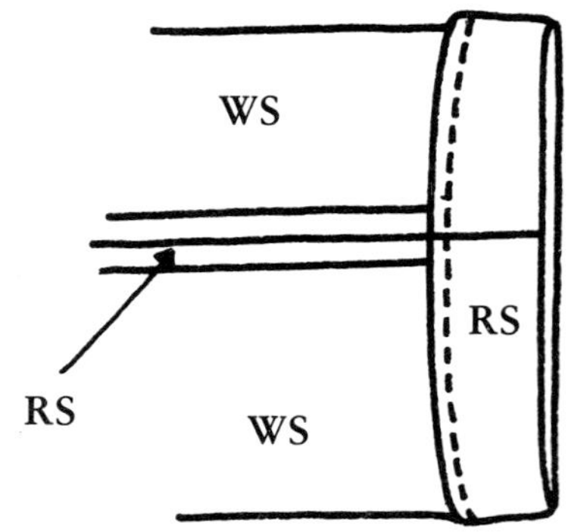

fig. 47

Slide the tunic under the machine and stitch on the line with a straight stitch, zig-zag stitch, or a stitch to match the one at the neckline.

10. Press the tunic. Roll back the sleeves to form cuffs if you wish.

Tunic with lacing

1. With the tunic cut out but still folded along the shoulders (pattern 1), make a cut 10cm long along the fold of the left shoulder only (fig. 48).

fig. 48

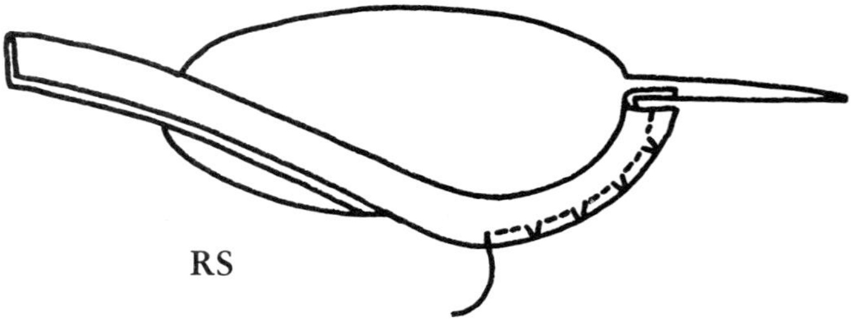

2. Using pre-folded braid insert the raw edge of the neckline between the layers of braid and tack. Start at the end of the shoulder open fold the braid at the neck corner so that it lies flat and ease the braid around the neck. On reaching the end of the shoulder opening cut the braid so that the two ends are level and turn under the raw edge of the braid on the right and wrong sides of the tunic. Hold the ends down with small tacking stitches(fig. 48).

3. Slide the tunic under the machine foot right side up and machine along the edge of the braid with a wide zig-zag stitch, blind stitch or an open embroidery stitch making sure the stitch falls on the braid but the needle goes just over the edge of it.

fig. 49

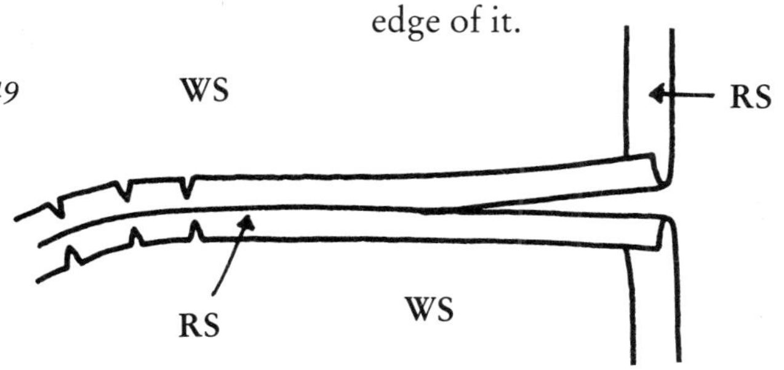

Follow steps 4-8 for plain tunic (page 48 to 50), but before stitching the left side seam mark a point on the seam 25cm above the hem, and when stitching that seam stop at that point and reverse the stitching to fasten off. Press and snip the seams as described for the plain tunic and press the hem. Move the tunic so that the slit in the left seam is on the ironing board, fold back the seam edges 1.5cm and press well. At the hem these seam edges fall on top of the hem. Press the corner well. Insert Wundaweb in the hem and along both edges of the slit and press well. Alternatively tack the edges and machine along the hem and up both sides of the slit using the same stitch as for the neckline. A third alternative is to attach braid to the edges of the slit in the same way as the neckline (fig. 49).

After pressing the tunic attach four or five pairs of eyelets to the shoulder opening and side slit. Lace them up either with cord, leather thonging or coloured boot laces, or make a metre-long piece of rouleau from fabric and use half of it at each opening (fig. 50).

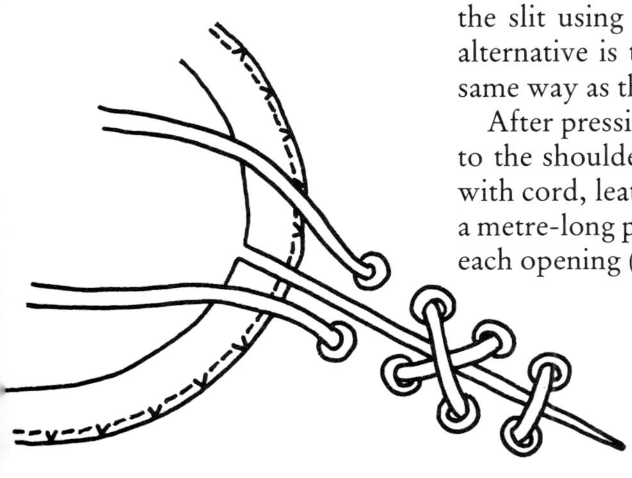

fig. 50

THE SKIRT (pattern 2)

This is a full gathered skirt which is easy to make. It has only one seam and elastic in the waistband. Attach pockets if you wish. You will need 2.3m of fabric 115cm wide. Choose soft cotton, polyester cotton or broderie anglaise. The fabric can be printed or striped, or it can have a border along the edge.

You will also need two reels of Drima or Duet and a piece of elastic webbing 3cm wide to fit round the waist and enough for a join. The pattern shown is for a skirt measuring 70cm from waist to hem when finished. Make a note of your waist measurement before you start.

Cutting out

1. Trim both ends of the fabric so that they are exactly on the straight grain. Press the fabric.
2. Fold the fabric in half with the right side out bringing the selvedges together at both sides. If the layers slip apart insert a few pins around the outside to hold them together.
3. Measure 75cm from the selvedge along the fold and make a chalk mark. Measure more if you are tall and need the skirt longer than 70cm when finished. If you are using a fabric with a border you may want to cut the skirt longer and trim off any unwanted part of the edge. Border fabrics often have 6-8cm of plain colour or unfinished print that you would not want to use (fig. 51).
4. Measure the same distance along the cut edges of fabric and snip. Cut from here right across the fabric to the chalk mark at the fold. If you are not confident of keeping straight then make several chalk lines in between to guide you.

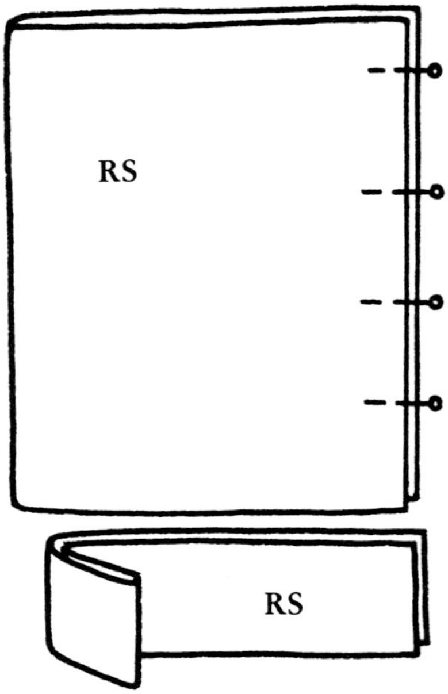

fig. 51

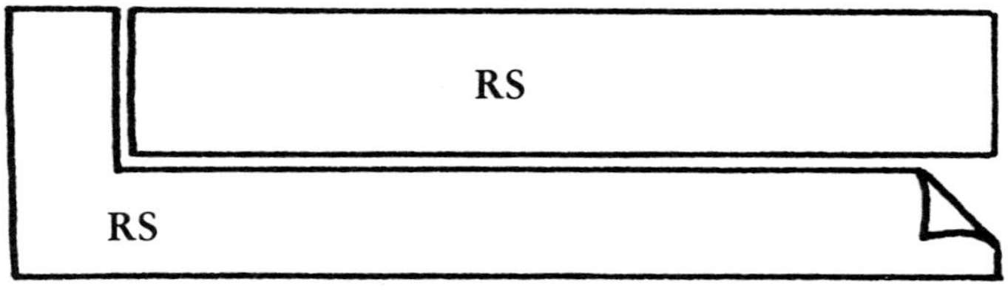

fig. 52

5. Fold the cut fabric over once and put aside.
6. For the waistband open out the remaining fabric so that it lies on the table singly and right side up. Draw a rectangle 9cm wide with one edge on the straight grain of the fabric and, in length, make it one and a half times your waist size. Cut out (fig. 52).

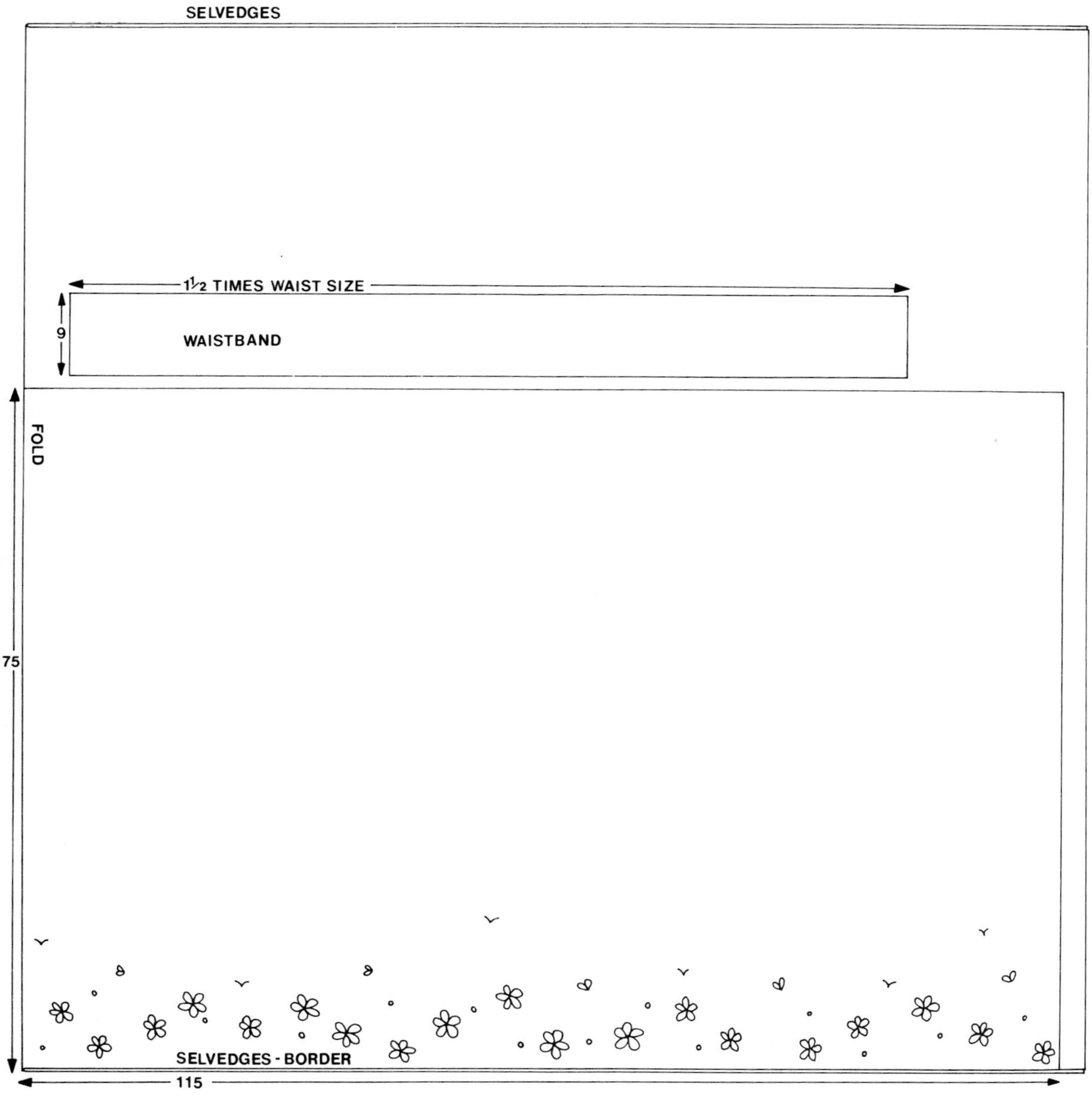

pattern 2. Skirt

Making the skirt

Make two patch pockets as described on page 76. If you are using fabric with a border design cut two matching pockets accurately, perhaps with the main part of the border along the top of each.

1. Fold in half the piece of fabric you have cut for the skirt with wrong sides together, measure 20cm in from the fold

and 10cm down from the waist edge. From that point rule a chalk line 10cm long and another down from the end at right angles about 10cm long. This marks the position for one top corner of one pocket. Transfer the mark for the second pocket by refolding the fabric with the wrong side out, line up the edges then bang sharply with your hand along the chalk lines (fig. 53).

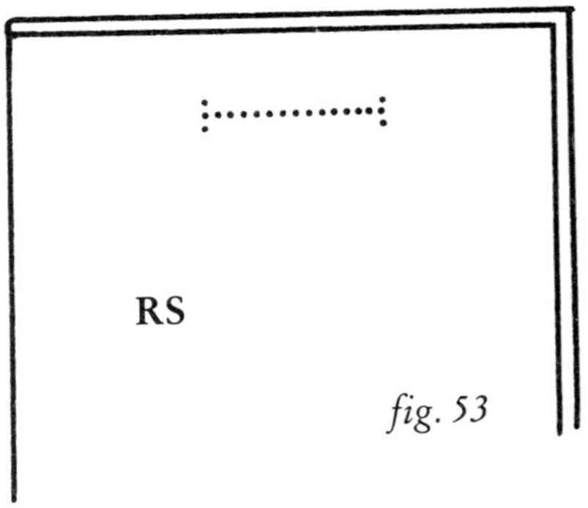

fig. 53

2. Open out the fabric, arrange it right side up on the table, pin the pockets in position and attach as described on page 78.

3. Fold the fabric into four and press the crease at the waist edge. Set your machine to the largest straight stitch and insert gathering threads along the waist edge, putting a line of stitches in each quarter of the skirt. Stitch 1.5cm in from the edge and start and finish 2cm from the ends. Leave the thread ends free at one end of each line of stitching but reverse to fasten off at the other.

4. Neaten both the vertical raw edges of the fabric with a medium-width zig-zag stitch.

5. Fold the skirt right sides together, put the two neatened edges together flat on the table and pin. Insert the pins at right angles to the edges about 12cm apart, starting at the hem edge and keeping the pin points facing into the fabric.

This seam can now be tacked if you wish but if there is a border pattern to be matched you should leave in the pins otherwise the upper layer of fabric will move when machined (fig. 54).

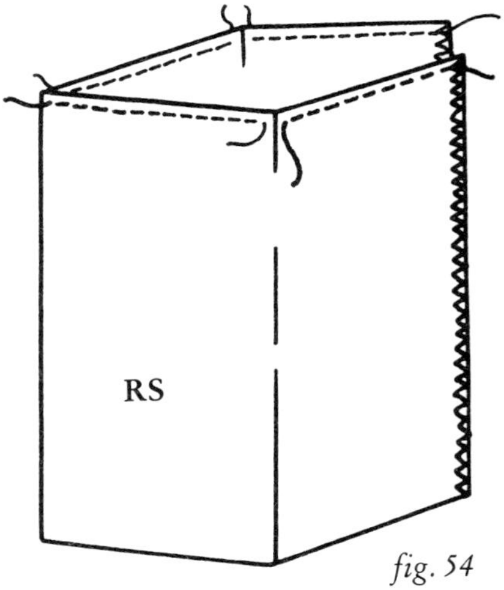

fig. 54

6. Stitch the seam with a medium-length straight stitch starting at the hem, stitching 1.5cm from the neatened edges and sewing slowly over the pins. Reverse the stitching at both ends to fasten off the thread. Remove the pins and tacking stitches (fig. 55).

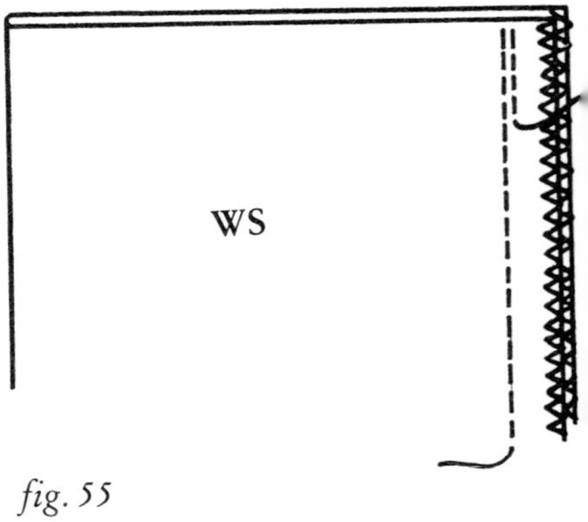

fig. 55

7. Place the skirt on the ironing board and press the stitching. Open out the skirt and slide it onto the board wrong side up and with the seam running straight along the board. Use the toe of the iron to open the seam edges carefully then press more firmly right along the seam. Turn the fabric over and press the seam on the right side.

8. Decide on the length you require the skirt to be. This can most easily be done by measuring a similar skirt you already have. Add 1.5cm and measure that distance from the waist edge towards the hem; make a mark with chalk. Slide the skirt onto the ironing board with the wrong side up, fold

over the edge until the chalk mark is on the edge and press. Measure the amount turned up then turn up the remainder of the hem the same distance and press the fold.

fig. 56

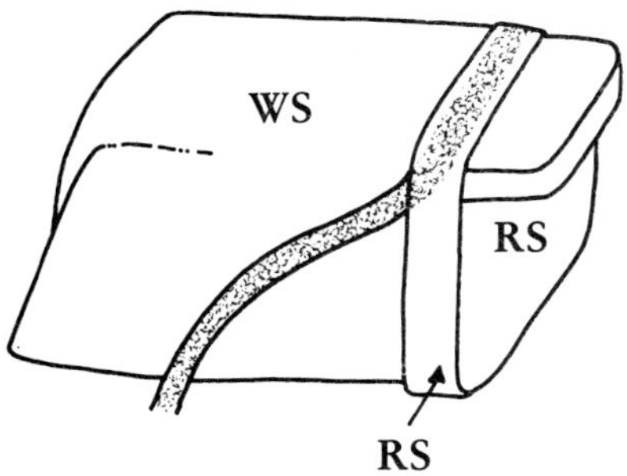

THE HEM

Complete the hem in one of the following ways:

Wundaweb (fig. 56) Trim down the edge of the fabric leaving only 2.5cm above the pressed fold. Neaten the raw edge with a medium size zig-zag machine stitch. Put the skirt back on the ironing board and press the zig-zag stitching. Arrange the hemline with the 2.5cm turned up. Slip a length of Wundaweb under the edge making sure it is covered by the edge of the fabric. Press well using a damp cloth.

Machine stitching Work a medium size zig-zag machine stitch over the raw edge to neaten it. Press the stitching. Tack the hem edge to the skirt. Turn the skirt right side up and mark a line on which to machine, measuring an even distance from the edge of the skirt, and making sure the stitching will fall about 5mm inside the zig-zag stitch on the under side. With the right side up machine on the markings using a medium straight stitch or a zig-zag or decorative stitch. Press the hem.

Hand stitching With the skirt wrong side up on the ironing board turn under the raw edge of the hem and press. Keep the hem depth even. Tack the hem just below the fold. Finish by working slip hemming in the fold. Press the hem.

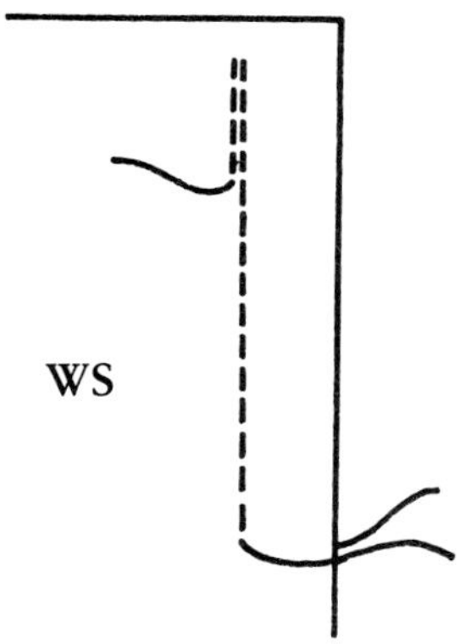

fig. 57

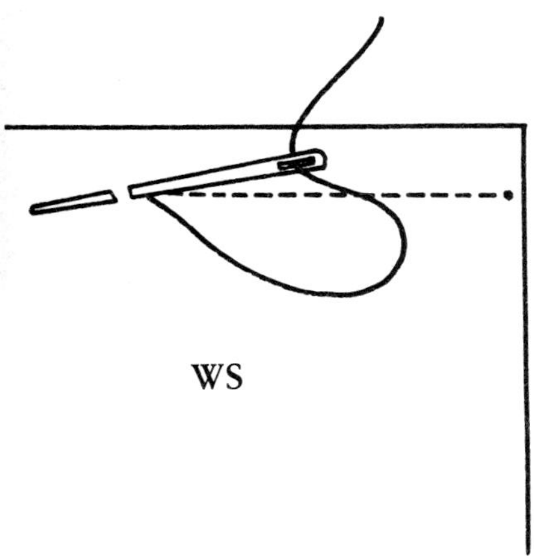

HOW TO PUT IN GATHERING THREADS (fig. 57)

Material is ruched or gathered to make it smaller and to provide fullness. The fullness may be for movement or for a bigger part of the figure or it may be just decorative. To draw up, or gather, put in a length of thread parallel with the edge that you want to gather. The stitch you use can be hand running stitch or needle running. Use a piece of thread equal in length to the fabric edge, put a knot in the end and insert the line of stitches 1.5cm within the edge; leave the end of thread loose, not fastened off. If you have mastered your sewing machine it is quicker to put the thread in by machine. To do this set the stitch to the longest straight stitch it will do. Slide the fabric under the needle with right side up and lower the foot with the needle 1.5cm from the raw edge. Reverse a little way to anchor the threads then stitch forward. At the far end stop machining. Do not reverse.

Points to remember:
Never make gathering threads too long. Stop at each seam, leaving ends, and start again 1cm further on. With the gathered skirt on page 53 fold the skirt waist into four and press creases at the edge about 10cm long. Open out the skirt and insert four separate gathering threads along the waist edge, one in each quarter of the skirt. When joining on the waistband, divide that also into four and start by pinning the quarter points together. This will also help in keeping the gathered area evenly drawn up.

In fact even with a short piece it helps to find the centre of the gathered section and the centre of the flat piece, pin the two together, pin the ends together and only then pull up the gathering thread.

fig. 58

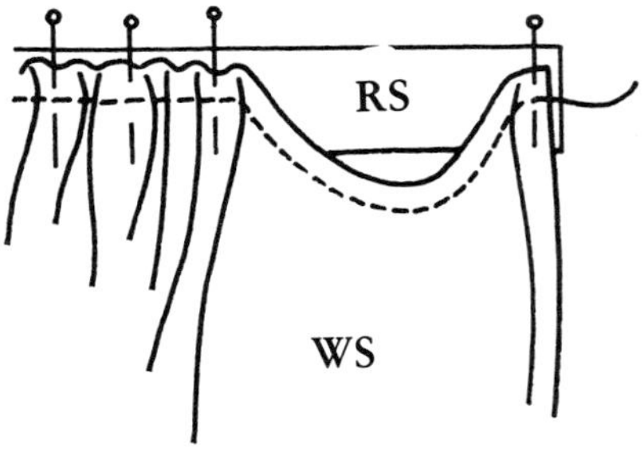

PULLING UP GATHERING THREADS

Hand gathering is easy to pull up, simply take hold of the free end of the thread and ease the fabric along it gradually. Move each bunch of gathers up to the next pin and then beyond. Hold the end of thread you are pulling at a point close to the fabric. Continue easing and moving the gathers until the section at the far end near the knot has sufficient gathers in it to allow it to lie flat against the ungathered piece to which it is pinned. Even out the gathers in that section so that they are not bunched together (fig. 58).

Insert pins across the gathers but pick up only a small amount of both layers of fabric under the gathering thread itself. Tack the fabric layers together making the stitches a fraction below the gathering thread. Fasten off the tacking. Remove the pins.

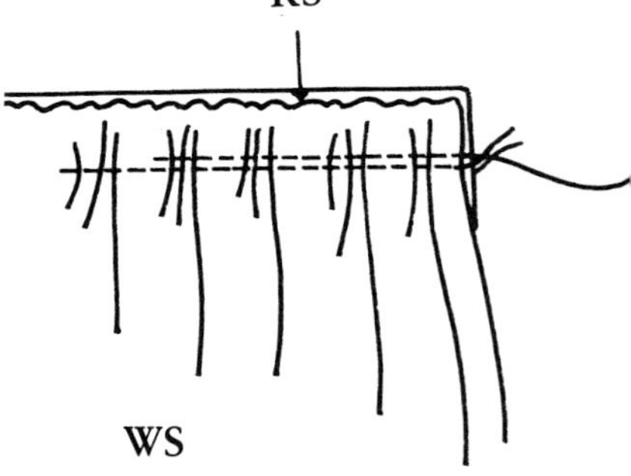

fig. 59

Proceed to ease up gathering into the next section, even it out, pin and tack as before. Continue until you reach the final section but here, after pulling up the gathered fabric to fit, you will need to anchor the thread to hold it firm. The easiest way to do this is to wind it round and round the pin nearest to it. Complete the pinning and tacking, then machine close to the tacking (fig. 59).

To pull up a gathering thread put in by machine take hold of the end of thread that came from the machine bobbin; it will be the one on the wrong side of the fabric. If you always insert the thread from the right side you then know that you always pull up the end on the underside. Machine threads produce firmer and more even gathers. Ease the fabric along the thread and pin and tack the sections exactly as described above.

MACHINING OVER GATHERS

Having taken the trouble to make the gathers they could then be spoilt by careless stitching so set the machine to a straight stitch that is larger than you have been using on seams but not as large as the gathering thread. Slide the fabric under the machine needle with the gathered section uppermost. Make sure the layer of fabric beneath is flat. Lower the foot and stitch between the tacking and the gathering thread. Stitch slowly, a few stitches at a time. Keep stopping to check the under layer of fabric because it can easily become caught up in a fold in the stitching. Also watch the gathers themselves. It helps to hold a bodkin in your right hand as you stitch to separate any gathers that bunch or form pleats and to ease them under the foot.

Remove the tacking stitches. Remove the gathering threads. Those inserted by hand can be removed by pulling the knot. To remove machine gathers snip the stitches at the end where it was reversed then pull on the other end of the thread, the same one used for easing up the gathers, and it will come out easily.

fig. 60

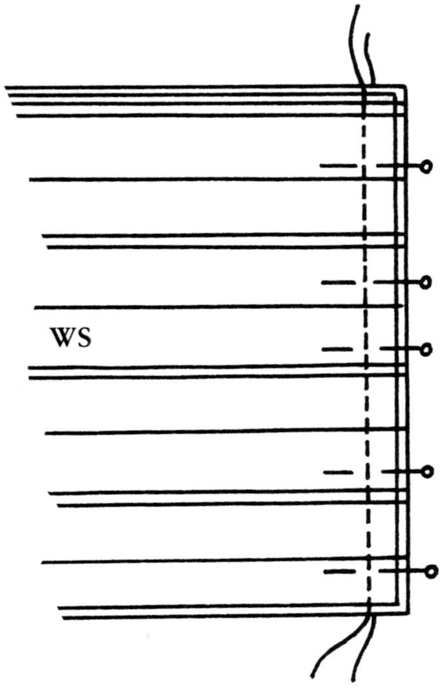

HOW TO MATCH THE PATTERN AT THE SEAMS

If you are using check or striped fabric or a border print that must be matched at the seams, arrange the layers of fabric right sides together then lift and fold back the upper layer so that you can see the design. At each stripe or point to be matched, carefully put back the upper layer and immediately insert a pin at right angles to the edge of the fabric. Have the head of the pin extending beyond the fabric edge and pick up a very small amount of fabric on the pin at a point 1.5cm within the edge (fig. 60).

Stitch the seam with edges and therefore pin heads to the right. Use a medium to large straight stitch on the machine and sew slowly over the pins, or, if you are nervous of doing this the first time, remove each pin as you come to it. Finish and press the seam in the usual way.

THE WAISTBAND

Cut the length of elastic to fit round the waist firmly and add 2cm for joining the ends.

1. Fold the piece of fabric with the right side inside and the

ends together. Tack across the end then machine or back stitch by hand from one edge but stop, reversing the stitching when halfway across. Do not remove the tacking stitches but press the join open (fig. 61).

2. Fold the waistband down the middle with the wrong side inside and press the edge. Fold the band equally into four and press the creases (fig. 62).

Also fold the waist of the skirt equally into four and re-press the creases made earlier.

3. With the skirt inside out match up each pressed crease to a crease in the waistband and pin together. The skirt is now pinned to the waistband in four places.

4. Work on one quarter at a time and pull up the free end of the gathering thread, easing the fabric gently along the thread. Even out the gathers, using your fingers, along the entire section as far as the next pin. When the gathered fabric is the same size as that section of the waistband and lying flat, wind the thread end firmly round the pin (fig. 63).

Even out the gathers again then hold them in place on the waistband by inserting about six pins along the section. Tack the section, make the stitches close to the gathering thread but below it, fasten off the tacking. Remove all the pins.

5. Repeat this sequence of gathering, pinning and tacking on the other three sections of the skirt. When the entire skirt is gathered and tacked to the waistband, arrange it over the free arm of the machine with the skirt uppermost and the waistband beneath. Use a fairly large straight stitch and machine round the waist. Stitch slowly, stopping often to check that the fabric is flat under the gathered section. While you stitch watch the gathers themselves; try not to let large pleats of fabric accumulate as it goes under the needle.

When you have stitched right round, overlap the stitching by 3-4cm to fasten off securely.

Remove the skirt from the machine. Pull out all the tacking stitches (fig. 64).

6. Trim the raw edges above the gathers to a width of less than 1cm. Set the machine to a medium zig-zag stitch and use it to neaten the edges, stitching over both edges together.

7. Press the skirt. Press the waistband so that it extends but do not flatten the gathers (fig. 65).

8. Remove the tacking stitches from the join in the waistband. Attach an elastic threader or a large safety pin to

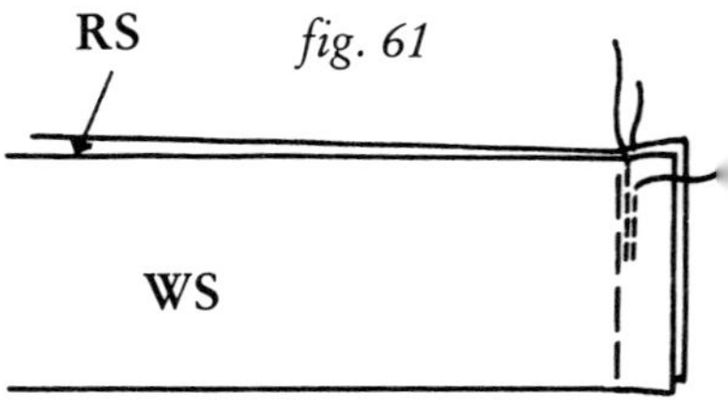

fig. 61

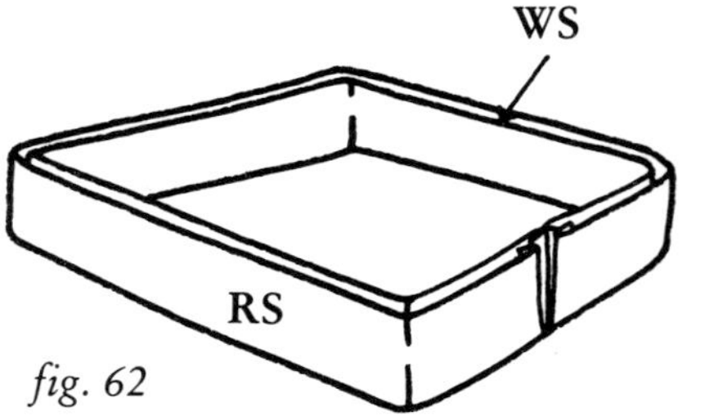

fig. 62

fig. 63
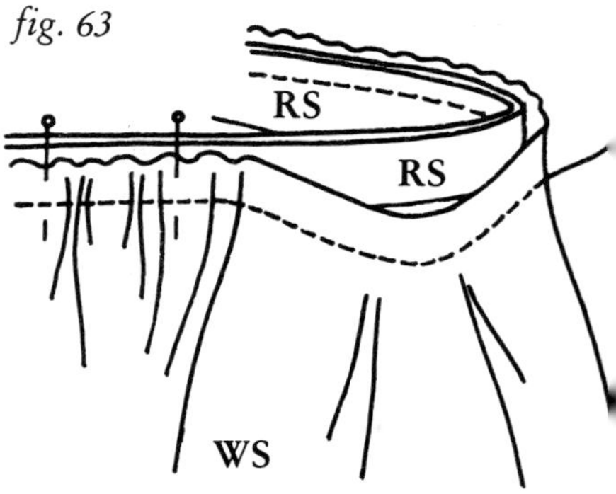

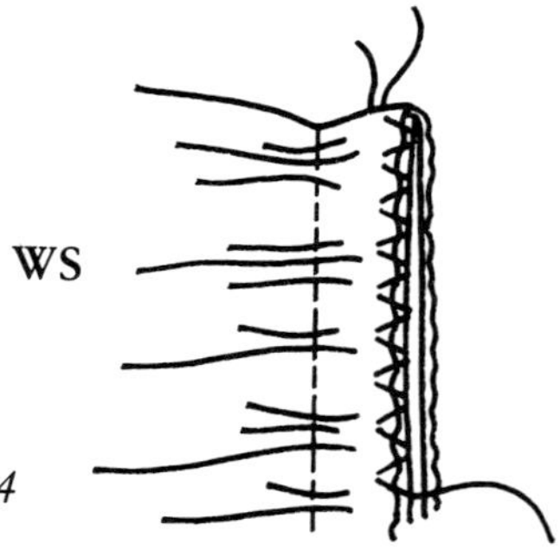

fig. 64

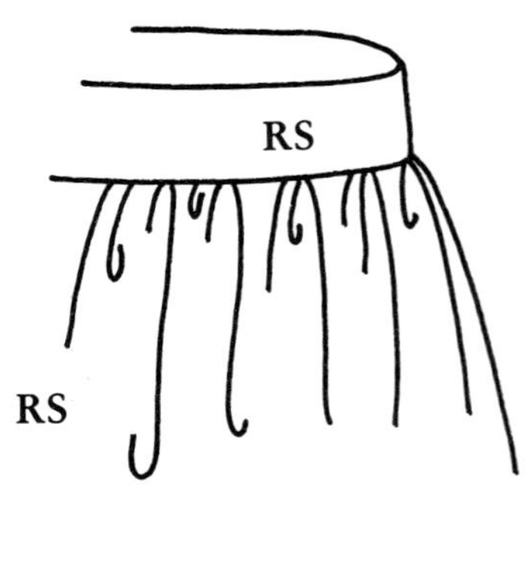

fig. 65

one end of the elastic and thread it through the waistband. Pin the free end of the elastic to the skirt to prevent it from pulling right through (fig. 66). Keep the elastic flat and untwisted. Ease the fabric along the elastic and pull the end free. Lap one end over the other and pin, overlapping the edges by 1cm. Cut a piece of tape or bias binding or trim a narrow strip of selvedge from your surplus fabric and put it across the elastic. Move the pin to one side then zig-zag twice to join the eleastic, sewing through the tape and both layers of elastic (fig. 67). Fasten off the stitching.

9. Ease the elastic into position inside the waistband. Close the gap in the waistband by oversewing the folded edges together.

fig. 66

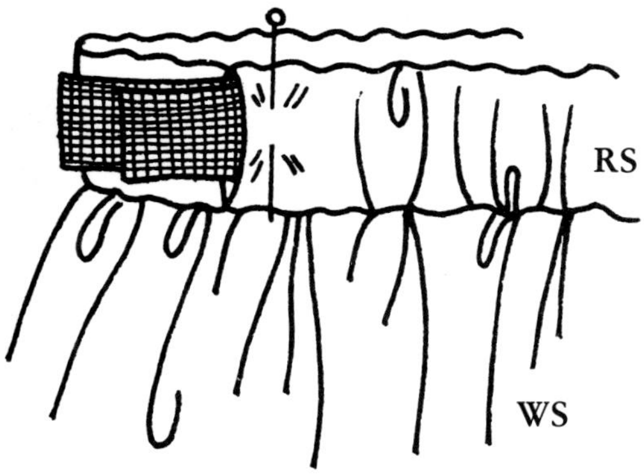

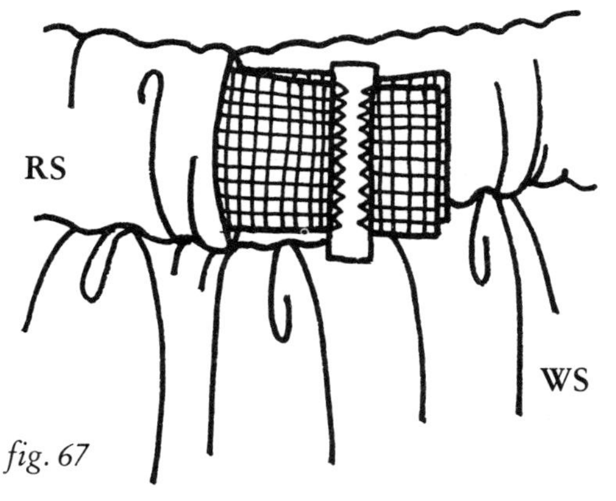

fig. 67

THE TROUSERS (pattern 3)

Easy trousers with elastic waist, straight legs and no side seams. Use the same pattern to make shorts by cutting off the legs below the crotch line at the length required.

You will need: 275cm of fabric 115cm wide, (choose soft striped cotton, brushed cotton or soft denim)
2 reels Drima or Duet
1m or 1 pack of Wundaweb
a length of elastic or elastic webbing 2cm wide to fit round your waist plus enough for a join

Cutting out

The pattern shown is for trousers with an inside leg seam

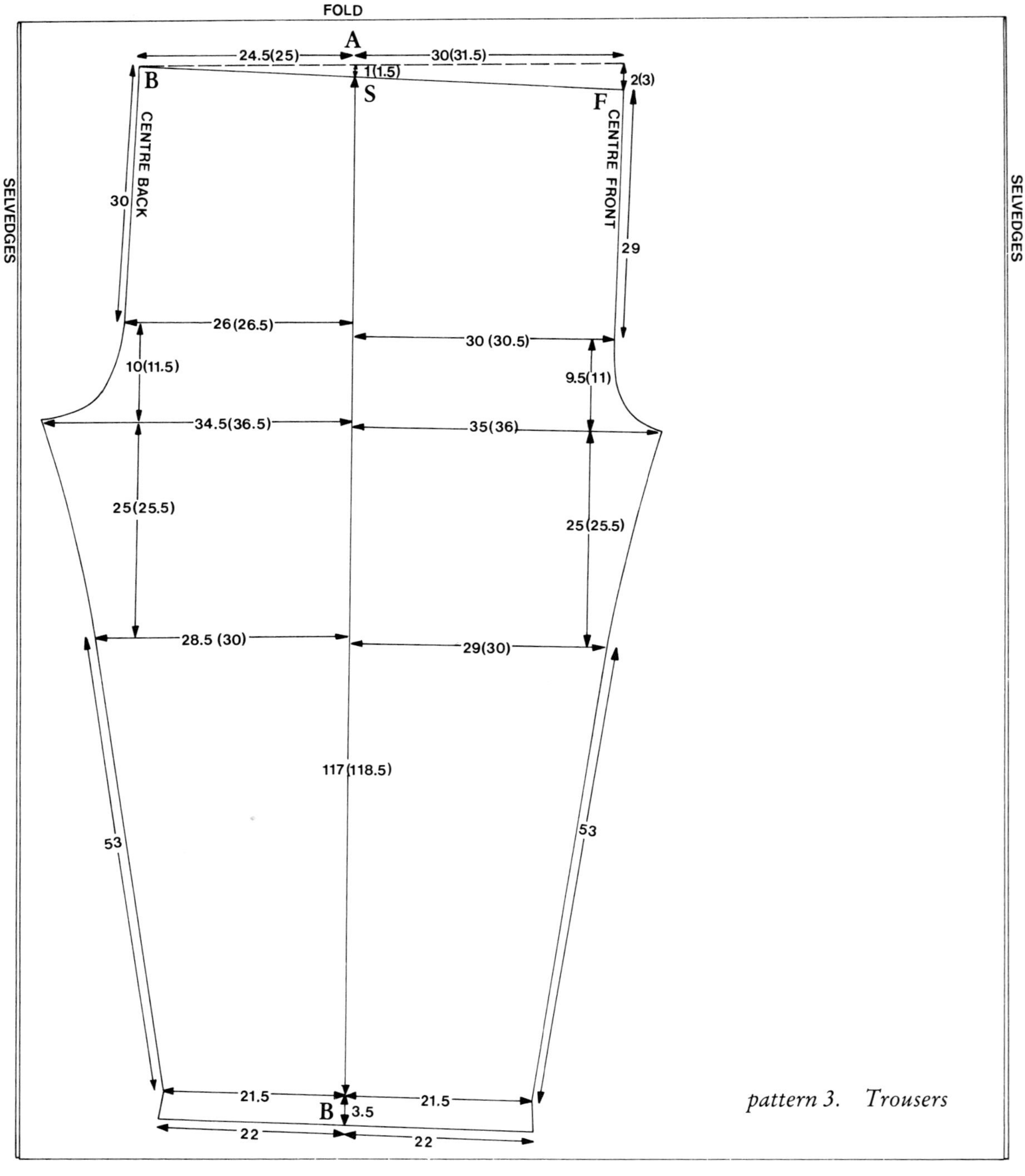

pattern 3. Trousers

length of approximately 72cm. If you are tall you will need to make the pattern longer at the hem. Measure the inside leg seam of a pair of existing trousers to find out what length you need them. You may prefer to make this pattern for future use in paper or, for a more durable copy, in light sew-in Vilene, or you can mark the trousers directly onto the fabric.

1. Fold the fabric in half across the width and lay it down with right side out and selvedges together.

2. First rule a long line, A–B using tailor's chalk and a ruler, parallel with the selvedge and approximately 45cm in from it. The line should be 121.5cm long for size 10 and 123.5cm long for size 12 (from now on size 12 will be shown in brackets). From A mark a point 1cm down.

3. At one end rule a broken line across the top at right angles extending towards the selvedge nearest to you by 24.5cm (25cm) and in the other direction by 30cm (31.5cm). From this last point measure 2cm (3cm) down and chalk the trouser waist edge from there across to the far end. The line slopes and should pass through the 1cm point at the middle. Mark the lower end F (front) the upper one B (back) and the middle S (side).

4. From point A measure and mark a series of points on the centre line A–B and rule lines out at right angles towards back and front to lengths given below.

Measure down from A 30cm, mark the point and rule a line out towards the back that is 26cm (26.5cm), long.

At 40cm (41.5cm), rule a line 34.5cm (36.5cm) long.

At 65cm (67cm), rule a line 28.5cm (30cm) long.

5. Join these points carefully to form the back crotch seam and inside leg. When making shorts mark off the length required on the inside leg seam.

6. Next, from point S on the A–B line, measure and mark a series of points and rule lines at right angles towards the front to lengths given below.

Measure from S 29cm: rule a line towards front that is 30cm (30.5cm) long.

At 38.5cm (40cm) rule a line that is 35cm (36cm) long.

At 63.5cm (65.5cm) rule a line that is 29cm (30cm) long.

7. Join these points carefully to form the front crotch and inside leg.

8. Finally complete the lower section of the leg by ruling a line at B to extend 22cm on each side to meet the inside leg

seam which should be 56.5cm long from the previous point. Draw the hemline 3.5cm above this to the length shown and complete the inside leg seam.

Cut out on the chalk line. Move the surplus fabric away. Fold the top layer of fabric over right side inside until inside leg edges are together. Insert several pins through two layers at right angles to hold the seam together. Lift the top trouser leg out of the way by folding it over. Pin the seam of the second leg in the same way, folding it right sides together (fig. 68).

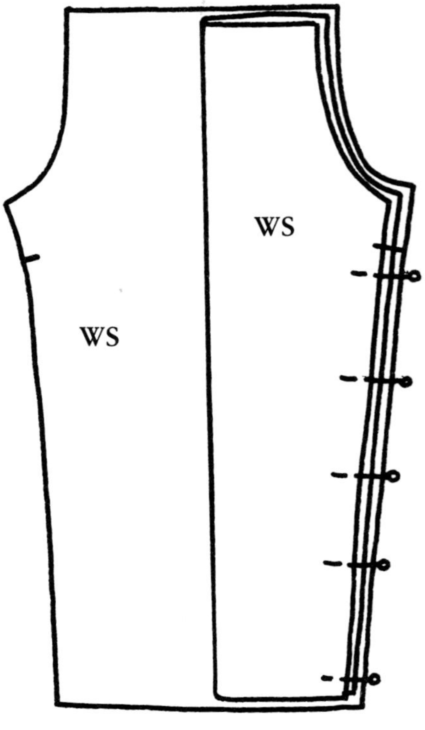

fig. 68

Making the trousers

Tack both the trouser seams starting at the crotch and stitching towards the hem. This is a long seam so keep the fabric flat on the table for accuracy. Remove the pins.

1. Put each seam in turn under the machine and stitch 1.5cm from the edge starting at the crotch and ending at the hem. Reverse to fasten the thread. Remove the tacking stitches.
2. Place each trouser leg on the ironing board with the seam flat and press the stitching. Revolve the leg until the seam is on top and in the middle of the leg. Press the seam open. Do this by opening the seam allowances with the fingers of your left hand and using first the toe of the iron and then using the iron flat but without too much pressure. It is all too easy to press too hard which will result in an imprint of the seam appearing on the other part of the trouser leg. Try to avoid this by pressing lightly but pressing several times. Turn each leg right side out, lay it on the ironing board and press along the seam again (fig. 69).
3. With the trouser legs right side out put the two leg seams together at the crotch. The fabric will be right sides together at that point; hold the seams together with a pin.

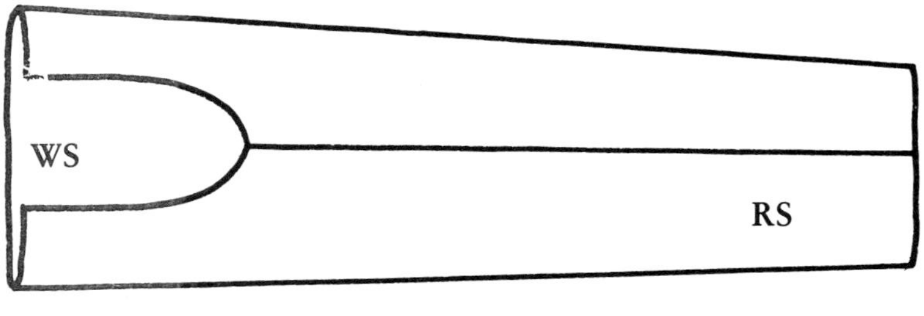

fig. 69

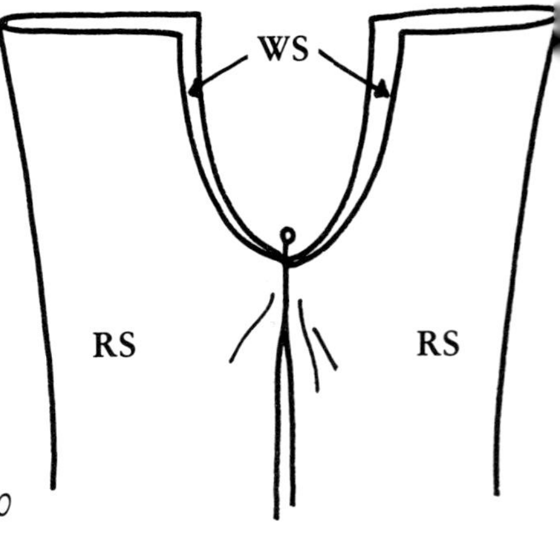

fig. 70

fig. 71

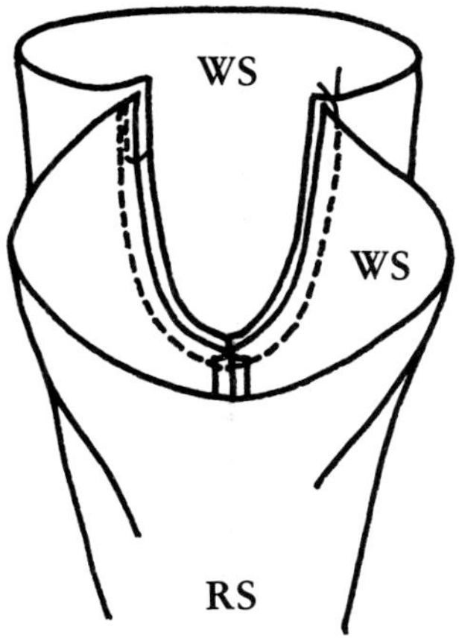

Move to the waist and pin the trousers together and do the same at the front waist. Take hold of the crotch seam and lift it, shaking the trousers so that the remainder falls out of the way to enable you to tack the seam from the front waistline, round the crotch seam and up to the back waist (fig. 70).

4. Remove the pins and machine the seam, holding the trousers so that none of the rest of the fabric becomes caught in the stitching. Fasten off the stitching. Remove the tacking stitches (fig. 71).

fig. 72

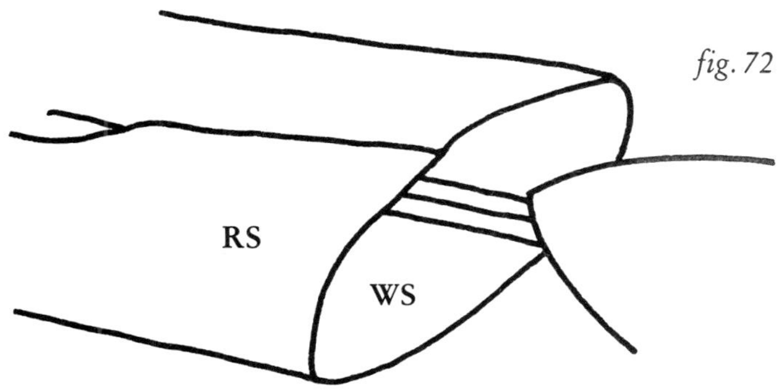

fig. 73

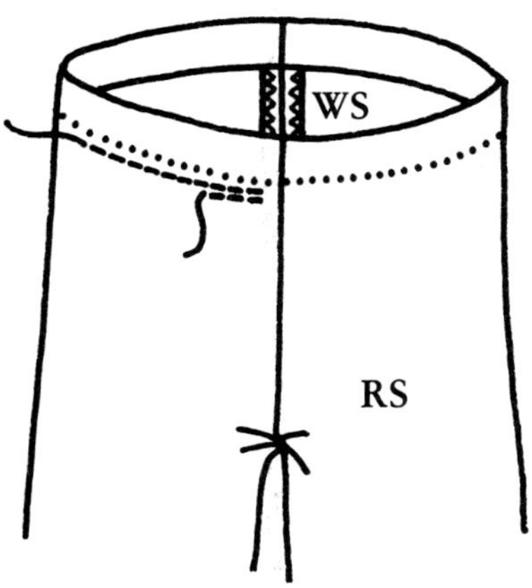

5. Slide the waist of the trousers over the end of the ironing board and press open the seam from the front and then the back as far down towards the crotch as you can reach with the iron (fig. 72).

6. Neaten each seam edge with zig-zag stitch. Neaten the waist edge of the trousers in the same way. Replace the waist on the ironing board fold over 3cm to the inside and press. Slide the trouser waist over the board right side up and mark a line 2.5cm from the edge with chalk or fabric pen (fig. 73).

7. Place under the machine foot and machine on the line with a straight stitch or a small zig-zag stitch. Begin at the back close to the seam, reverse to fasten the thread, stitch round the waist but stop and reverse again to leave a gap of 1.5cm in the stitching. Press the waist (fig. 74).

8. Measure the elastic round your waist and insert it in the trousers following instruction 8 for the skirt waist (fig. 75).

9. Put on the trousers and, wearing shoes, turn up the hems to the length you want, inserting several pins to hold up the surplus! Take off the trousers and put one pin firmly at the lower fold of each leg; remove all other pins. Lay the trousers out on the table with the inside leg seams together and check that they are the same. Adjust if necessary.

fig. 74

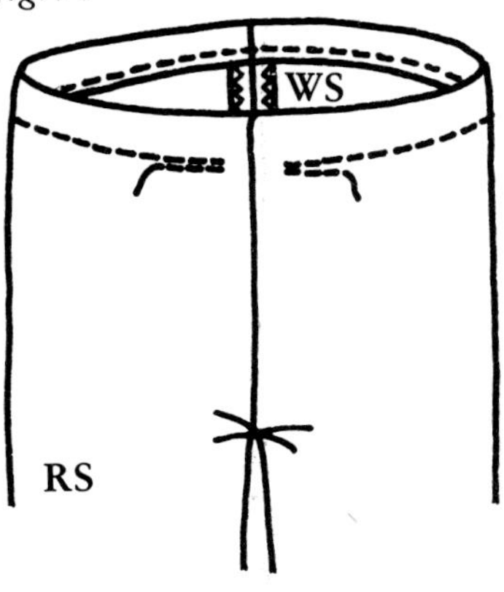

10. Turn up each hem to an even depth all round measuring carefully and tacking near the fold. Arrange each hem on the ironing board and press this tacked edge.
11. Turn the trousers inside out and trim off the surplus fabric to a depth of 2.5cm from the fold.

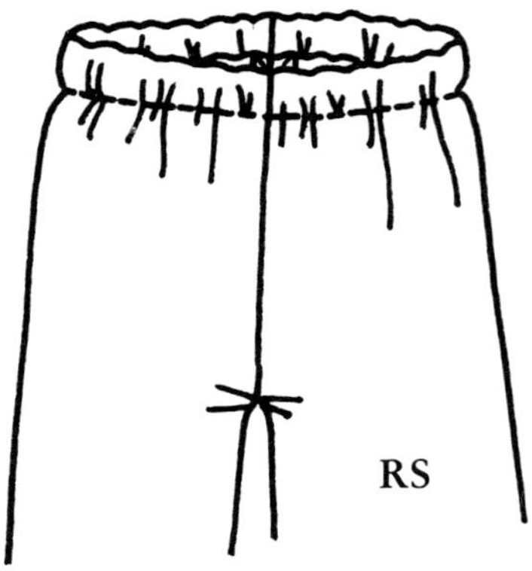

fig. 75

Complete the trouser hems by one of the methods described for the skirt.

TROUSER CREASES

If you want creases in your trousers or shorts press them in place after stitching the waist edge but before inserting the elastic.

Hold up the trousers by the hems, with both legs together. Revolve the legs until both seams are together and in the centre. Still holding the hems like this lay the trousers on the ironing board keeping the seams together from the hem right up to the crotch. Smooth out all fabric on each side (fig. 76).

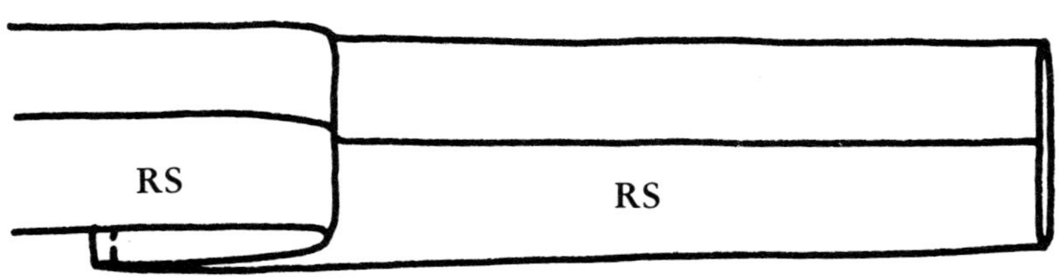

fig. 76

Lightly press across the legs at the hem and for 20cm or so up the leg. Carefully fold back the upper leg as far as the crotch. Press a firm crease in the leg beneath, starting at the hem and pressing up towards the front waist. Repeat on the back but do not try to make the crease extend to the waist. Keep the fabric of the leg as smooth as possible while you press.

Fold the upper leg back into position on top. Take hold of the entire pair of trousers but without disturbing either of the legs, and turn them over. Fold back the upper leg, which is the one already pressed, and press the one underneath.

Hold the trousers up by the waist and check that the creases are straight and sharp. Re-press the legs after completing the hems.

THE SHORTS (pattern 3)

These are easy to make and have an elastic waist. Use the trouser pattern to the length you want. Measure the length of a pair of shorts you have in the wardrobe. Measure at the side from the lower edge of the waist finish down to the hem. Take another measurement at the inside leg from the crotch seam to the hem. Make a note of both measurements adding 6cm to each for hems and seams.

To make the shorts you will need 60cm of fabric 115cm wide, one reel of Drima or Duet and a waist length of elastic webbing 2cm wide.

Cutting out

If you have already made the trousers you will find it easy to follow the illustration and draw the pattern of the shorts on your fabric. If you have made a pattern for the trousers in paper or Vilene all you need to do is trace off the upper part for the shorts and pin it on the fabric.

If you are drawing the pattern directly on your fabric, follow the instructions below.

1. Fold the fabric in half across the width with right side and selvedges together. Make sure any lines or stripes are level and on top of each other.
2. First rule a long line A–B as shown, parallel with the selvedges and about halfway across the fabric. Make this line equal to the measurement you took from your own shorts at the side, including the extra 6cm. As a rough guide this line is likely to be between 30cm and 50cm in length. Below a point A mark a point S (SIDE) on the line.
3. Rule a line at right angles across the end of this line. Mark off a point 24.5cm size 10 (25cm size 12) towards the selvedge nearest to you and mark off a point 30cm (31.5cm) in other direction.

From this last point measure 2cm (3cm) down and draw the shorts waistline from there to the far end of the guide line. The line slopes and should pass through the points. Mark the end of the line F (FRONT) at the lower end and B (BACK) at the higher end.

4. From point A measure and mark a series of points to be joined to form the front and back crotch and leg seams. Begin with the back. Measure down from A 30cm and rule a line towards the back that is 26cm (26.5cm) long. Measure

from A 40cm (41.5cm) and rule a line 34.5cm (36.5cm) long. Carefully join the points to form the curve of the back crotch.

Next, measuring from point S, measure down 29cm and rule a line towards the front of the shorts that is 30cm (30.5cm) long. At a point 38.5cm (40cm) rule a line that is 35cm (36cm) long.

Carefully join the points to form the curve of the front crotch.

5. Finally look at the measurement you took at the inside leg seam of your own shorts and measure that amount from the furthest point of the crotch curve on both the back and the front, holding your ruler in slightly at an angle. Mark both points then rule the hemline between these points and through the lower end of the original construction line A–B. If the three points are not in a straight line draw a gently curved hemline.

Cut out the fabric, cutting on the chalk line. Move the surplus fabric away; cut pockets from it if you wish.

fig. 77

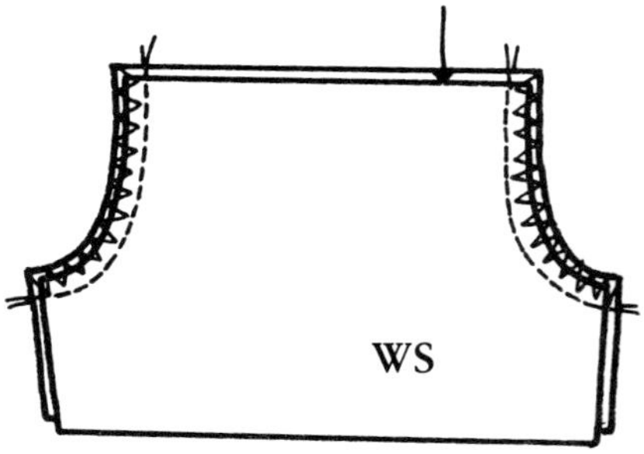

Making the shorts

If you wish to attach pockets, do so now, placing them either on the back or the front of each leg approximately in the middle and with the top edge 10cm below the waist edge of the fabric. If you think the pocket pattern as shown is too big in proportion to your shorts reduce the dimensions and make smaller pockets.

1. Neaten the edges of both pieces of fabric using a machine zig-zag stitch. Neaten the front inside leg and crotch seam, the waist edge and then the back crotch and leg seam.

2. Arrange one shorts leg on the table with the right side up and the other leg on top right side down. Begin at the front and put the two crotch edges together, insert two or three pins or tack. Move the top layer of fabric sufficiently to allow the back crotch edges to meet and pin or tack in the same way.

Put each of these seams under the machine and stitch with a straight stitch 1.5cm from the neatened edges (fig. 77).

3. Slide the shorts onto the ironing board wrong side up and press open both seams from the waist. As you reach the crotch curve use the toe of the iron to avoid creasing the fabric.

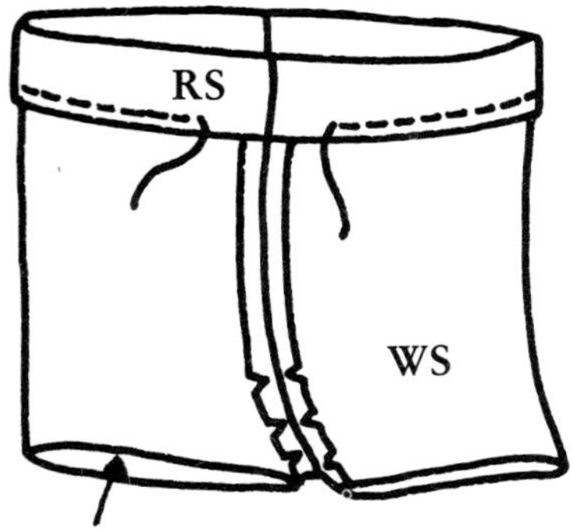

fig. 78

4. With the shorts still in position fold over the waist edge 3cm and press the crease all round. Turn the shorts right side out, put the waist back on the ironing board, tuck under the pressed edge and using chalk or fabric pen mark a line a distance of 2.5cm from the waist edge.

5. Slide the waist edge under the machine needle right side up and stitch on the line with a straight stitch or a small size zig-zag. For extra neatness begin at the centre back of the shorts, reverse to fasten the thread then sew round the waist. When you are almost round stop and reverse again, leaving a gap of 1-1.5cm in the stitching (fig. 78).

6. Next, with the shorts wrong side out put the two leg seams together. With the edges level place the two seams together, keeping the edges open and pin. Insert another pin halfway between the seam and the edge of the leg. Machine this seam, stitching 1.5cm from the edge and removing the pins as you reach them. Slide this seam onto the ironing board wrong side up and press it open (fig. 79).

fig. 79

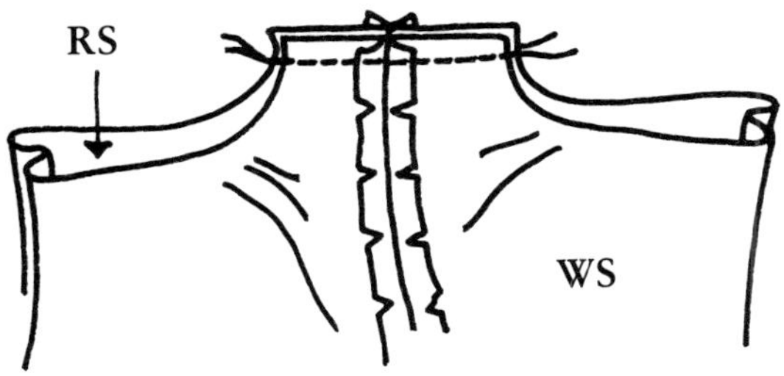

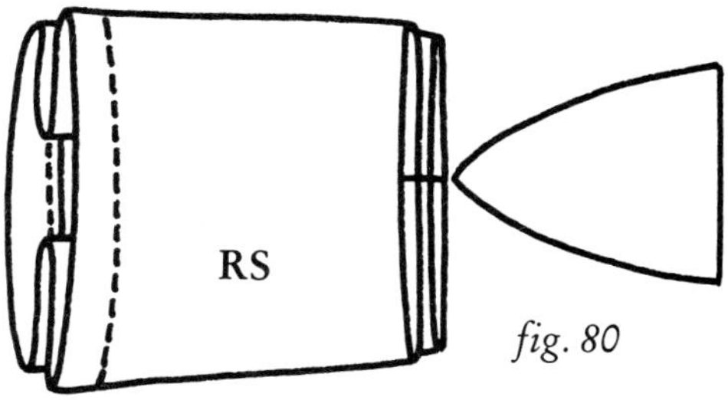

fig. 80

7. Move the shorts round on the ironing board and see if each leg will fit onto the board so that you can turn up and press 2cm all round each one. If the board is too big hold the leg up double, fold the edge over with your fingers, pull it taut and place each leg in turn flat on the board and double. Press by putting the iron in the middle of the leg hem, pressing both folds at once, then revolve the leg to press the remainder (fig. 80).

8. Finally, on the right side draw a line 1.5cm from the hem on each leg, and machine, or simply slide each leg onto the machine and using the guide line on the machine bed to stitch 1.5cm from the edge. Use a medium-size straight stitch or a small zig-zag stitch. If you are going to make the tunic to match the shorts make a note of the stitch you use or keep a small piece of fabric with some stitching on for reference. Press the shorts.

9. Measure the elastic round your waist and cut it to length allowing 2cm for joining. Attach an elastic threader or a rouleau needle to one end and insert in the top hem of the shorts and join.

(See instruction 8 of the skirt waistband.)

THE BELT

You will need:

- a spare piece of fabric
- a length of belt-stiffening, waist-size plus 12cm
- a slip-through buckle or a clasp
- 4cm of Velcro or 2 Velcro Spot-Ons

Making the belt

1. Measure the length and width of the belt stiffening and cut a piece of fabric the same length but twice the width plus 3cm. Make sure you cut accurately; use the selvedge of the fabric if you can.
2. Fold the fabric right side inside and press lightly. Insert pins at intervals at right angles to the belt to hold the edges together. Set your adjustable marker to the width of the belt stiffening plus 3mm and mark a line of dots that distance from the fold using a fabric pen or chalk pencil. Mark a line one end 1cm from the end (fig. 81).
3. Machine along the dots with a medium-length straight stitch, turn the corner at the end and stitch across the belt and reverse to fasten off. Press the stitches.
4. Turn the belt right side out; a rouleau needle can be used for this, or a knitting needle, or a ruler. Roll the seam between your fingers until you have worked it to one side and it becomes the edge of the belt. Press on both sides.

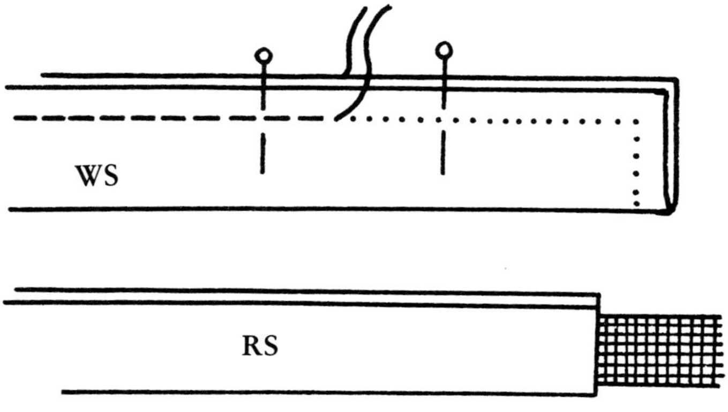

fig. 81

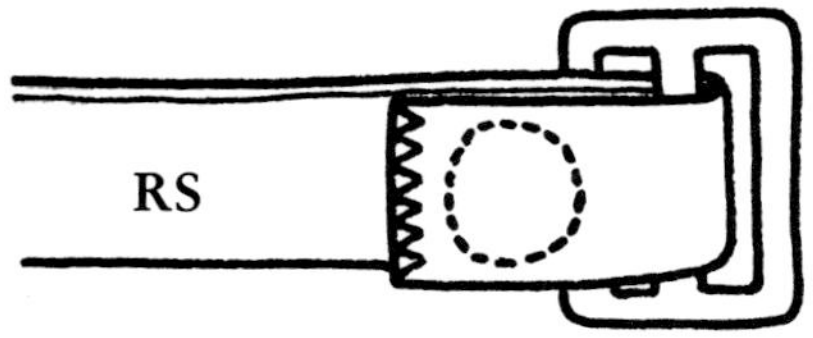

fig. 82

5. Slide the belt-stiffening into the belt. Stitch twice across the open end with a wide zig-zag stitch. Slip this end over the bar of the buckle, fold it back until it is clear of the buckle, hold it in place with a piece of basting tape and machine across the belt with a zig-zag stitch. Fasten off the ends by reversing. Try on the belt, fasten it to fit and mark the position of the free end. Sew the Velcro in that position. Use hemming stitch and attach the soft side to the end of the belt the hook side near the buckle. A Velcro Spot-On is easy to use, simply stick each half in position and stitch round. If instead you use a piece of Velcro, trim the ends neatly, put each piece in position, hold in place and hem round.

If using a clasp, thread one end of the belt over the bar, fold it back 4cm and hem across the end firmly. Thread the other end over the other end of the second piece of clasp, try on the belt and adjust the end to fit. Mark the position of the end and take off the belt and hem a piece of Velcro in place to hold the end back so that the belt is adjustable.

Note: If you wish to use the clasp on other belts use Velcro on both ends of the belt (fig. 82).

THE WAISTCOAT (pattern 4)

A short sleeveless self-lined jacket to make by hand or by machine. The lines of quilting are easy to do and provide some excellent stitching practice. The waistcoat edges are bound; you can use purchased bias binding or you can make your own using the same fabric or a contrast.

Fabric

You will need 80cm of fabric 115cm wide and 3m of binding, or 1m of fabric if you are using self fabric for binding the jacket. Choose soft printed cotton or crisp moiré taffeta if you are going to do machine quilting. Choose soft wool or satin if you are going to quilt it by hand.

You will also need two reels of Drima or Duet and 40cm of wadding. See page 73 for quilting instructions.

Cutting out

1. Fold the fabric across the width with the right side out so that the selvedges are together. Insert a few pins at the selvedge and two or three along the fold of the fabric.

2. At the fold, which is the centre back of the waistcoat,

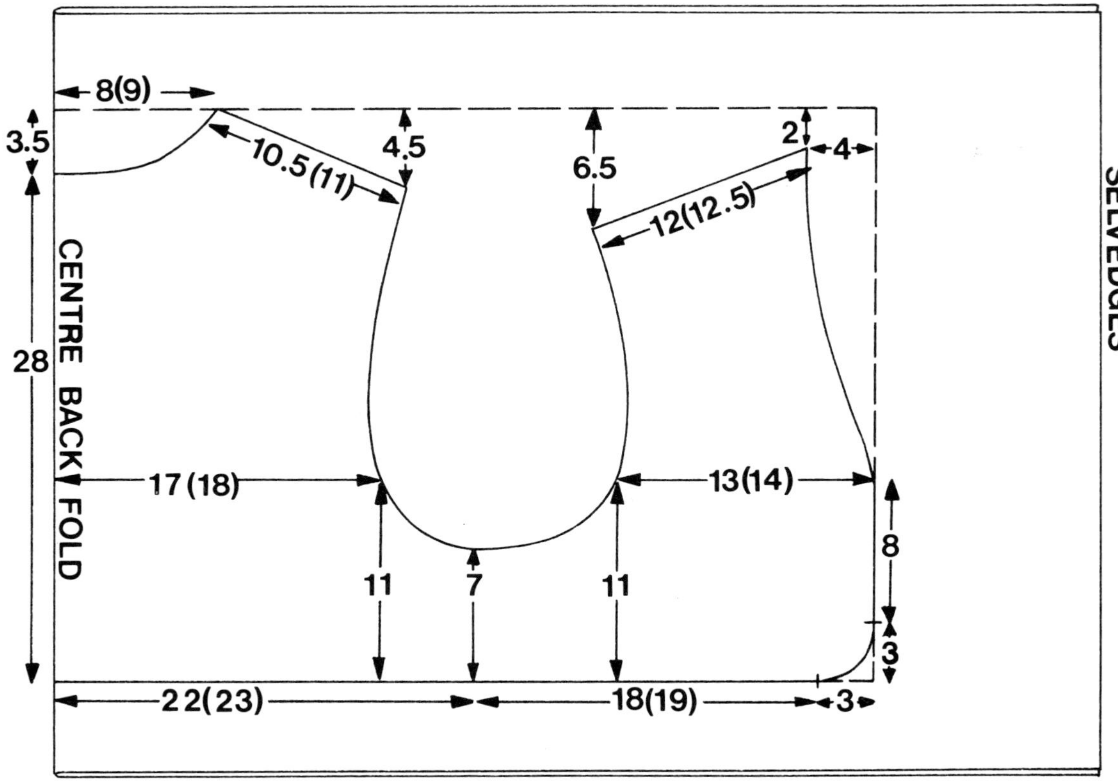

pattern 4. Waistcoat

mark two points 31.5cm apart and rule chalk lines at right angles across the fabric.

3. On the lower line, which is the hemline, mark off 22cm (23cm), rule a line 7cm long at right angles. This is the base of the armhole. Mark a point 21cm (19cm) further on and complete the rectangle.

4. Measure 11cm up from the corner for the base of the neckline and curve the bottom corner of the waistcoat as shown marking off 3cm points as a guide.

5. Draw the lower part of the armhole by measuring in from the centre back and centre front the distances shown, at a point 11cm above the hemline.

6. Draw the back neckline by measuring 3.5cm down the fold and 8cm (9cm) along the horizontal line and then draw a shallow curve as shown.

7. Finally draw the back shoulder seam by swinging a line 10.5cm (11cm) long until it meets a point exactly 4.5cm below, following the measurements given. The front shoulder seam is a little longer than the back and will be eased to fit.

9. Complete the back and front armhole and the front neckline with gentle curves. Cut out the fabric.

The pattern has to be cut twice, one piece forming the lining. Quilting must be worked before the waistcoat is cut out as the stitching will contract the fabric. Mark and cut out the pattern once for the lining and lay it on top of the remaining piece of fabric matching the folds carefully. Chalk round the outer edge marking the size onto the fabric below. Remove the lining.

Transfer the outline to the under layer using dressmakers' carbon paper and a tracing wheel. Fold the paper with the right side out and slide it between the layers of fabric. Trim off some of the surplus fabric to make it easier to handle by cutting round the waistcoat outline at least 6cm outside the line.

THE QUILTED WAISTCOAT (pattern 4)

Prepare a piece of bias binding 3m long. If you use purchased binding open out one fold and press it lightly to partially remove the crease.

If you are making your own binding cut and join sufficient 2.5cm wide crossway strips in matching or contrast fabric and pass it through a 12mm tape-maker.

1. Attach the binding to the armholes. Place binding right side down to the right side of the waistcoat with one crease of the binding in position 2cm from the edge of the fabric. Tack the binding in place round each armhole (fig. 83).

fig. 83

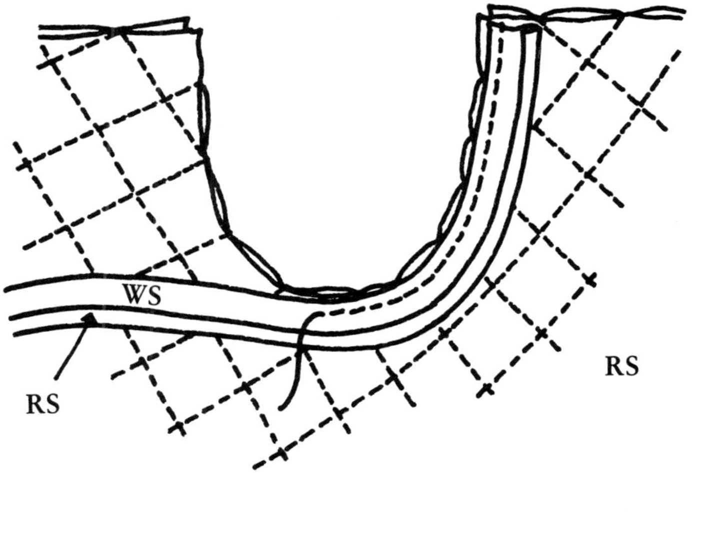

2. To sew by hand, work running stitch or back stitch along the crease of the binding. If you prefer to machine it, stitch along the crease with a medium length straight stitch. Press the stitching flat using the toe of the iron (fig. 84).

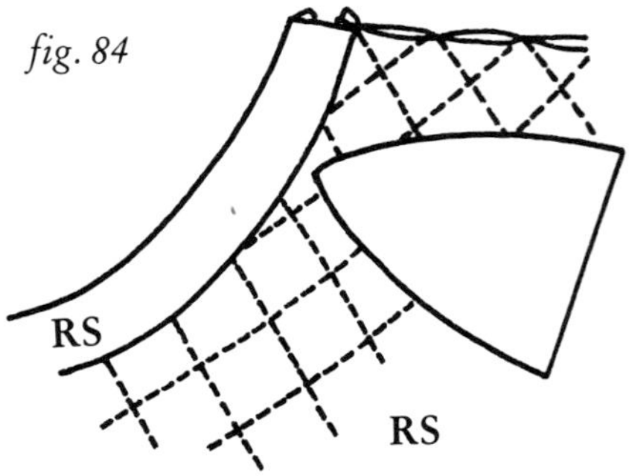

fig. 84

3. Trim off the edge of the waistcoat taking about 2mm from the binding as well. Arrange the waistcoat on the ironing board right side up and again using the toe of the iron, push the binding over the edge of the quilting so that it is right side up and extending beyond the waistcoat edge.

4. Holding the waistcoat with wrong side towards you roll the binding towards you and hold its folded edge exactly on top of the stitching. Tack the binding to the waistcoat. Insert the stitches near the edge of the binding but do not try to pass the needle right through all the layers. This is an example of surface stitching, often used where each subsequent layer needs to be anchored only to the layer beneath. Surface stitching is quicker and easier to do than deep stitching; it also reduces the amount of handling of the fabrics so you should use it wherever possible (fig. 85).

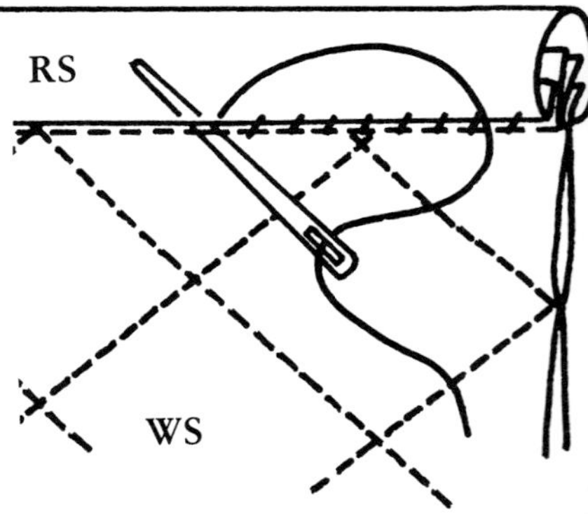

fig. 85

5. Sew the edge of the binding to the waistcoat using hemming stitch. Use short pieces of thread and a No. 7 needle, put a knot in the thread and tuck it under the binding with the first stitch. Hold the edge of the waistcoat at right angles to your body and work towards you inserting the needle at right angles to the edge. Make the stitches by picking up the thread of the machine stitch, or if you sewed it on by hand, a small amount of fabric under each stitch. Take the point of the needle immediately into the folded edge of the binding. This is an easy way of practising regulating your hand stitches especially if there are machine stitches to use as a guide because these stitches automatically ensure that your hemming stitches are neat and even-sized. On completing the hemming remove the tacking stitches and lightly press the binding on both sides of the waistcoat.

6. To join the shoulders of the waistcoat, fold the waistcoat front over the back with the right side inside. Hold the shoulder edges level and insert two pins to hold them together. Tack the layers together starting at the armhole edge to make sure the bindings are level. Begin by making two tacking stitches right over the edges of the binding then tack from there to the neck edge of the waistcoat (fig. 86).

7. Slide each shoulder seam under the machine foot and

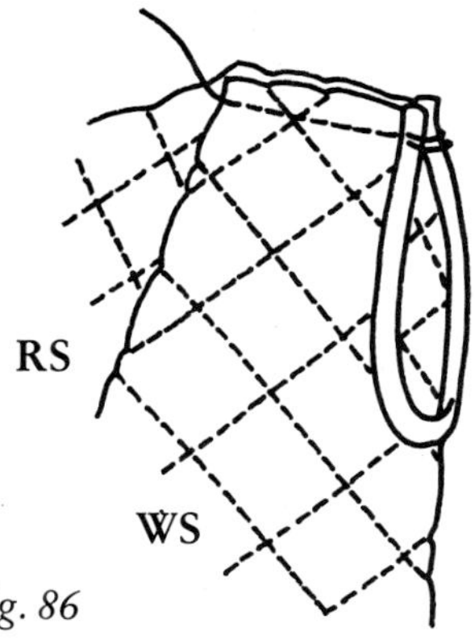

fig. 86

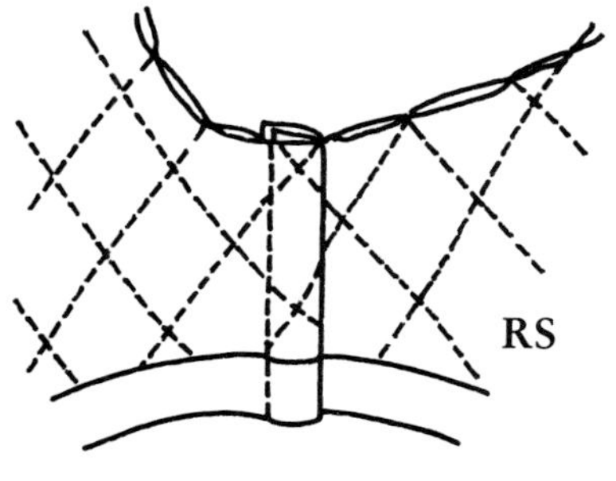

fig. 87

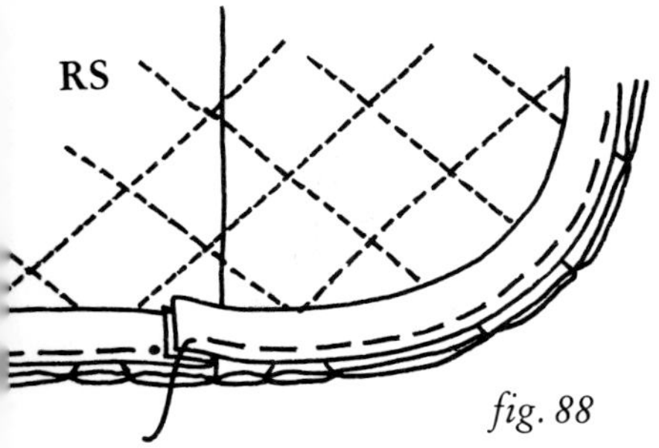

fig. 88

stitch with a medium-size straight stitch 1.5cm inside the raw edges. Reverse the stitching at each end to fasten off. Alternatively, back stitch the seams by hand. Remove the tacking stitches.

8. Trim the raw edges down to a width of about 6-8mm. Neaten them either by oversewing them by hand, taking the needle through both layers of fabric, or by machine using a wide zig-zag or other open zig-zag stitch.

A further alternative finish for these seams, which you can use if you have gained confidence in machining, is to stitch them again. Press both edges towards the back of the waistcoat then put the seam under the machine foot right side up and work a row of small zig-zag stitch, medium straight stitch or embroidery stitch parallel with the seam line and the width of the foot away from it (fig. 87).

9. After stitching the seams press them flat, make sure all thread ends have been cut off and then using a short piece of thread which matches the binding. Neatly oversew the three edges of binding together where the seam lies under the shoulder. Try to ensure that the seam edge is hidden inside the waistcoat.

10. Attach the binding to the remaining edge of the waistcoat. Start tacking it in place at one of the underarm seams, on the right side of the waistcoat, lining up the crease of the binding – 1cm within the waistcoat edge. On completing the tacking fold over one end of the binding and trim the end to 1cm then lay the other end of binding on top, trimming that also to 1cm. Take the final tacking stitch through these ends to hold them flat (fig. 88).

11. Machine or hand stitch in the crease of the binding. Trim the edges and press and stitch exactly as for the armholes. Remove all tacking stitches. Press the binding. Press the finished waistcoat lightly.

If you do not wish to quilt the waistcoat make it from two contrasting fabrics with the binding in a third fabric or contrasting purchased binding. Cut out the pattern in both fabrics and tack them wrong sides together, and follow steps 1-11 as for the quilted waistcoat.

Quilting

Lay the wadding flat on the table, open out the waistcoat fabric and place it wrong side down on the wadding. Use tacking thread and a No. 7 or 8 needle and work lines of tacking through fabric and wadding. Start at the centre back of the waistcoat and work towards the front edge then turn the fabric round and complete the lines of tacking on the other half. Next mark lines on which to quilt. Guide lines can be made with tacking stitches but you will find it quicker to use a fabric marking pen. Use the 'Fade-away' pen then the marks will disappear automatically. Use a ruler and mark a line of dots with the pen or tacking stitches, from the end of the shoulder seam across to the underarm point and beyond. Use your adjustable marker set at 7cm and mark several more lines parallel with the first (fig. 89).

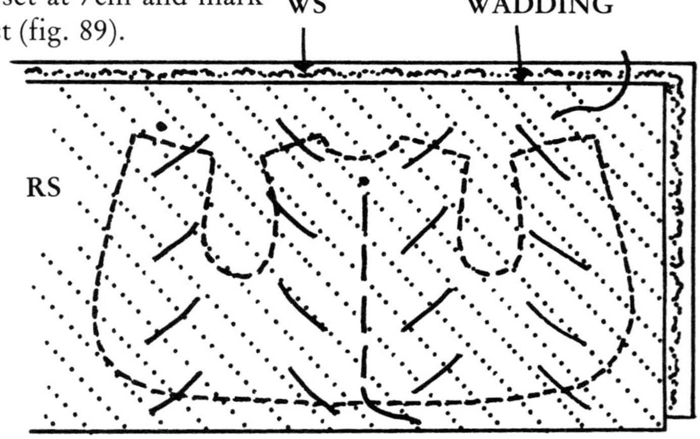

fig. 89

Start to quilt the fabric using a No. 8 needle and Drima or Coats' Quilting thread in matching colour; put a knot in the end. Begin by passing the needle between the layers to hide the knot, bring the point up on the end of one of the lines. The stitching can be done with running stitch but you will find it easier to make small stitches and to keep them evenly spaced if you use prick stitch. Stitch along all the marked lines with the fabric uppermost working in the same direction across the fabric; then mark a few more parallel lines and stitch those. Continue until the entire area has been

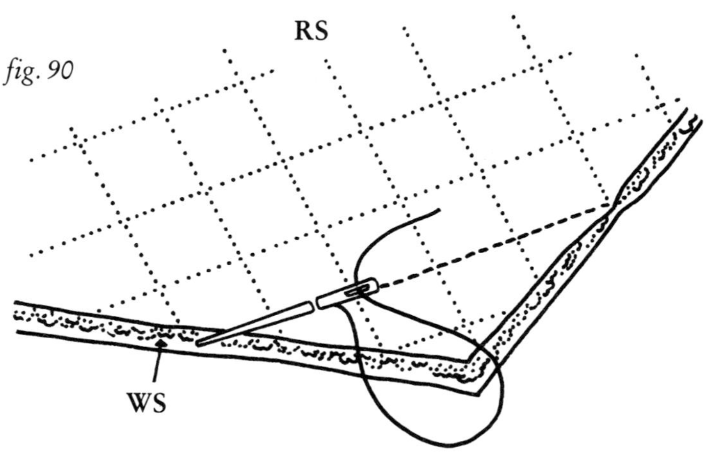

fig. 90

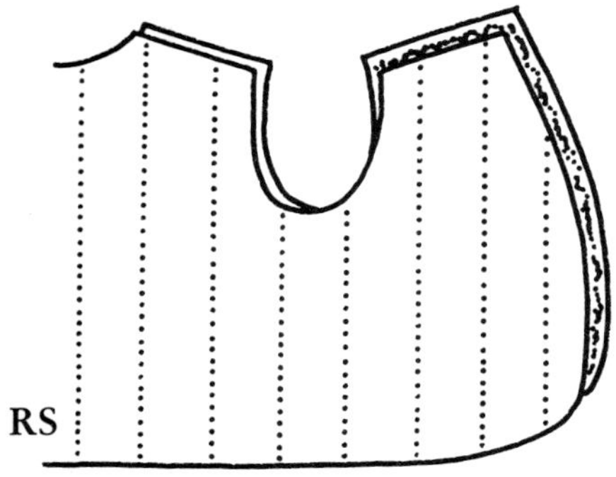

fig. 91

covered then mark and stitch parallel lines in the other direction to complete the pattern (fig. 90).

Note that you need not completely fill the armhole areas.

Tip If you are new to sewing you may find the hand sewing tedious although you should remember that it is excellent practice. To speed things up you can plan to quilt only certain areas. For example quilt only the back or only the fronts of the waistcoat. If you decide to be selective you could confine the areas by working vertical lines of stitching instead of diamonds (fig. 91).

PRESSING

Do not press the quilting but press the rows of stitching by smoothing the toe of the iron only along each line.

THE QUILTED BAG (pattern 1)

fig. 92

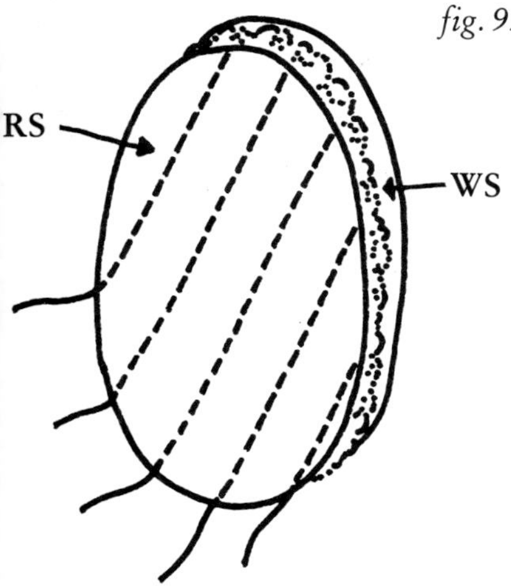

The bag can be made from surplus fabric left over from the tunic, or you can use any other fabric you have. On a piece of paper draw an oval the size shown in the diagram on page 99 and a second piece for the front of the bag, extending from the bottom up to the dotted line. Cut out both patterns. The larger piece represents the back and also the flap. You will need two pieces of fabric slightly larger than the oval and two more slightly larger than the bag front. The fabrics can be matching or contrasting. Cut them out but make them at least 2cm bigger all round than the pattern pieces.

Making the quilted bag

You will need a piece of wadding the same size as the bag pieces you have cut out, a reel of Drima or Duet and 250cm of binding or crossway strip for the strap and to bind the outer edge of the bag.

1. Place one oval piece of fabric wrong side up on the table with the wadding on top and the other piece of fabric on top of that wrong side down. Baste in lines up and down the fabric stitching through all the layers. Repeat with the other pieces of fabric.

Mark out a pattern for quilting in the same way as for the waistcoat. Work the quilting by hand or machine. Draw the correct size and shape on each piece and trim to size. Press lightly (fig. 92).

fig. 93

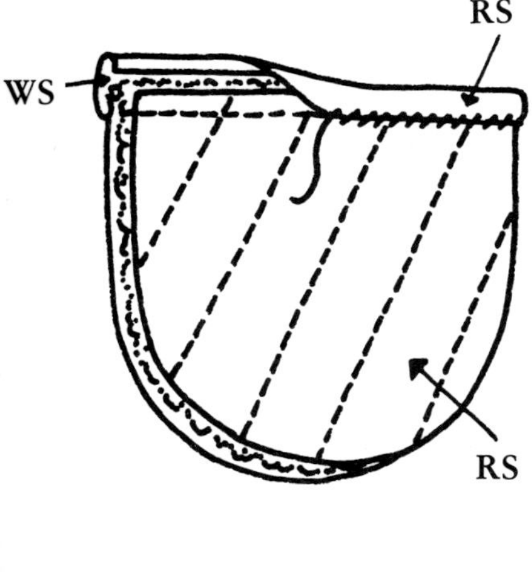

2. Attach binding to the straight edge of the bag front on the right side and finish it by hemming the binding to the bag on the wrong side (fig. 93).
3. Place the bag front on the main piece with wrong sides together and curved edges level. Tack together along the bound edge and round the outer edges.
4. Attach binding all round the outer edge of the bag, joining the binding neatly just below the edge of the bag front. Make the join by turning in the ends of the binding to meet each other, trim them and oversew together. Finish the binding by hemming on the inside of the bag (fig. 94).

Note that whichever side you attach the binding your final stitching will show so stitch very neatly.
5. To make the strap press the remaining piece of binding flat without creases. Fold it right sides together and press lightly. Machine down the length of the strip and turn it right side out with a rouleau needle, manipulate the join along the edge and press it with your fingers so that the join is along one edge and the rouleau is flat. Press the rouleau.
6. Attach the strap by turning under 5mm at each end and pinning it to the bag under the flap. Hem the strap ends firmly to the bag (fig. 95).
7. Fasten the bag by sewing one Velcro Spot-On to the middle of the flap, with the other half on the bag.

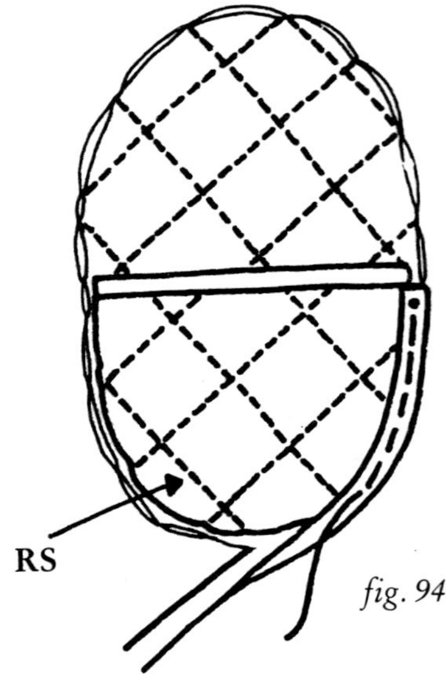

fig. 94

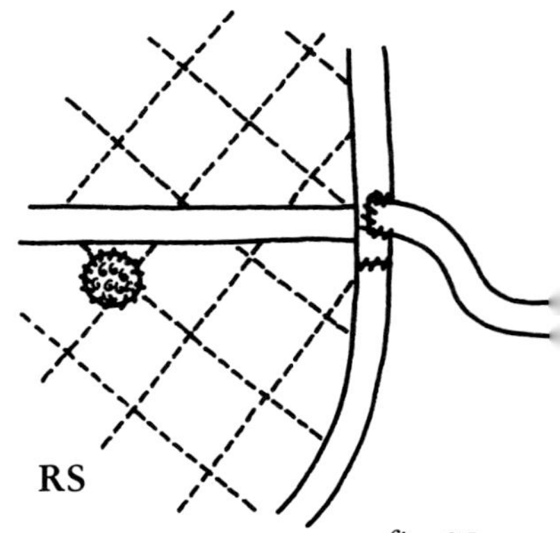

fig. 95

POCKETS (pattern 5)

The pocket illustrated can be attached to the skirt, tunic, trousers or shorts as a feature that is both useful and decorative. You can have one or two and you can have them on the front or the back or at the sides of any of the garments. Sew them on by hand or by machine.

The pattern and cutting out

The pocket could be drawn directly onto the fabric using tailor's chalk and a ruler but if you make a paper pattern you will be able to use it for more than one garment (fig. 96).

Draw a rectangle on a piece of paper 18cm x 16cm, cut it out and fold over one end 3cm; fold in the other three sides 1cm and crease. This is the pattern for a patch pocket. To make neat corners they should be mitred. Fold the corners into a mitre now and you will find it easier to follow the instructions when you make the mitre in the fabric.

pattern 5. Pocket

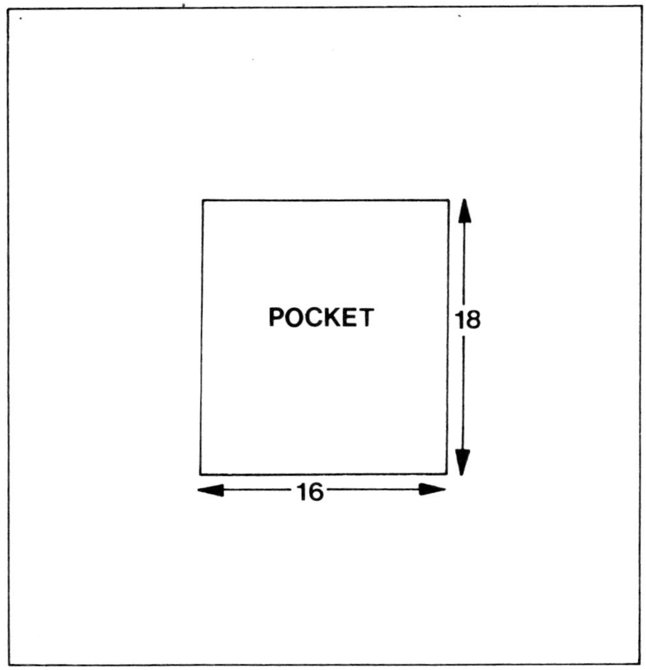

fig. 96

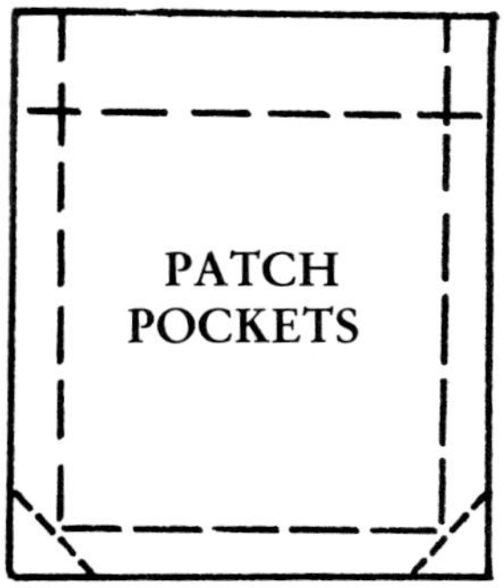

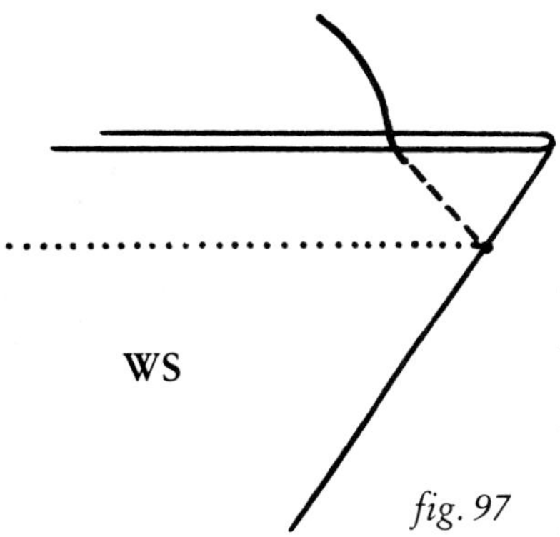

fig. 97

Open out the paper at the bottom corners, fold the corner of the paper over at an angle of 45 degrees, crease and open it out again. Fold the pocket with the two edges together and crease. The line on which you will stitch is the crease across the corner. Mark this on the paper with a clean line (fig. 97).

Write PATCH POCKETS on the pattern; write FOLD OVER on the crease at the top. Cut out. Pin the pattern to a piece of fabric with one edge on the straight grain or on a stripe or line on the fabric. Cut round the pattern, move the pins. Cut another to match if you want two pockets.

fig. 98

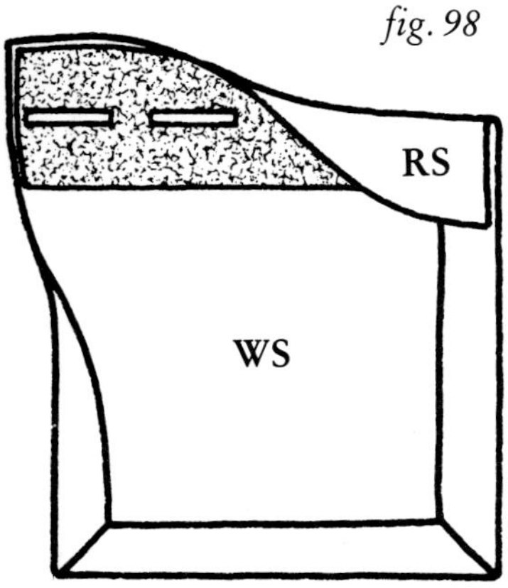

Cut a piece of light Fold-a-Band for each pocket to fit across one end. Place each piece on the wrong side of the fabric with one edge level with the edge of the pocket. Press the Fold-a-Band with a warm iron. Press it again using a damp cloth until it is firmly stuck. Fold over the top edge along the perforations in the Fold-a-Band and press. Turn in 1cm on the other edges and press. Open out the corners and press to form a mitre exactly as you did on the paper (fig. 98).

To stitch the mitre, open out the corners and fold the fabric with the wrong side out, stitch the crease using hand back stitch and sewing thread. Trim the fabric by cutting off the corner near the back stitching. Trim the pocket so that the corner turns right side out by pushing your thumb against it and folding the pocket over it. Make both corners the same way; arrange the pockets right side up on the ironing board, pull the corners square and press. Open out the top edge, turn the pocket over, fold in the side edge and press then fold down the top edge and press again.

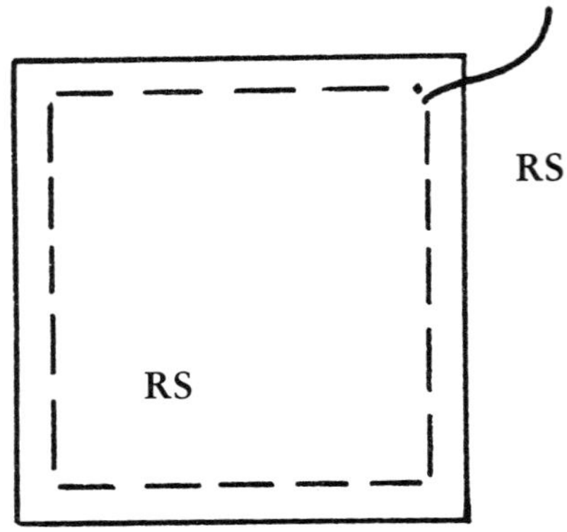

fig. 99

ATTACH THE POCKET

Place the pockets in position on the right side of the garment and anchor them with a few pieces of basting tape or pins. Tack round all four sides, stitching through the pocket and the garment (fig. 99).

Arrange the garment right side up. Sew by hand or machine (fig. 100).

fig. 100.
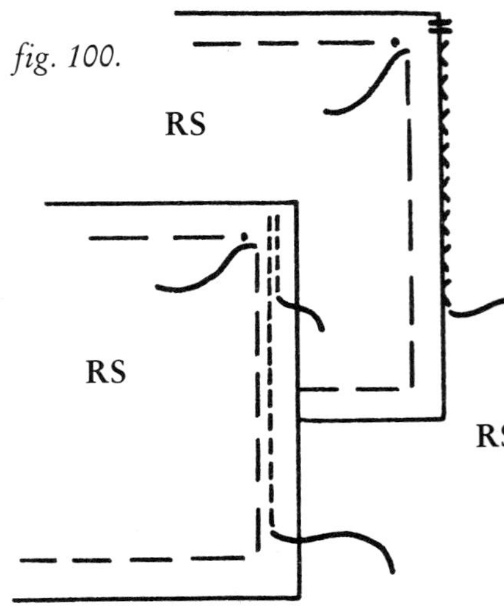

By hand: make small hemming stitches just under the edge of the pocket. Make a small bar tack at the top corners.

By machine: slide the fabric under the machine needle, use a small straight stitch and lower the foot so that its edge is level with the edge of the pocket. Stitch forward for three stitches then reverse for about four stitches then sew forwards all round the pocket, turn the corners carefully. At the final corner fasten off by reversing for four stitches.

Repairs

To make a patch or repair a tear or a hole use the same technique as for the pocket but cut the rectangle smaller. Trim the top fold of the pocket to 1cm, mitre all four corners place the patch in position over the hole and machine or hem all round. On the underside of the garment trim away the fabric to 1cm from the stitching. Turn under the raw edge and tack it to the garment, press, machine or hem. If you sew the patch by machine try using a medium-width machine zig-zag stitch to attach it. Make sure the needle clears the folded edge of fabric. Fasten off all ends of thread neatly. Cut off thread ends close to the fabric at the end of each row of stitching so that you do not have to trim again later (fig. 101).

fig. 101
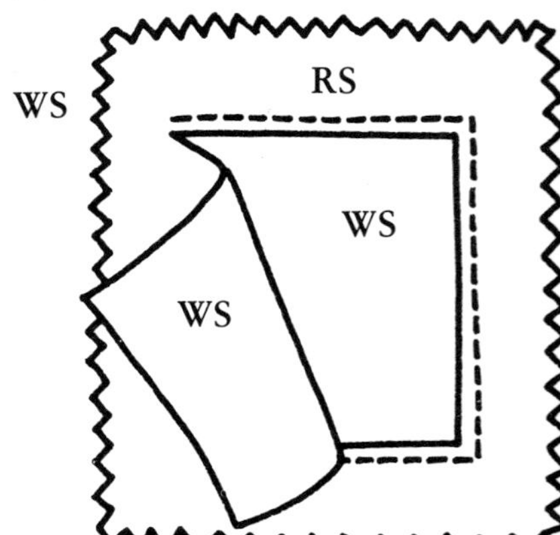

11 COMMERCIAL PAPER PATTERNS

These are patterns which are full size, usually printed and made of either tissue paper or a thicker paper. They are obtainable from shops and stores where either you select the style you want from a catalogue or select the pattern from a rack. Patterns are also frequently offered by mail-order through magazines or you will find specially designed patterns included with some books.

What size pattern

You must decide which pattern size is nearest to your measurements. The table on page 80 shows the appropriate body measurements for each normal dress size. If you fall between sets of measurements choose the smaller size because patterns allow ease for movement. The bust size is the most important because waist and hip size are easy to adjust when you try on the garment and fit it. Similarly the back waist length is easy to correct. You will soon know which size pattern to buy.

Depending upon where you obtain your pattern there may be some choice of proportion. For example the table on page 80 shows the measurements used for the category known as 'Misses' and most patterns for women are produced in this category. However, you will find a wider variety included in the catalogue of the larger pattern companies and you should consult the page in the back of the catalogue for other categories into which you might fit. There you will also find the size charts for men's, boys', girls' and children's clothes.

Misses patterns are designed for a well-proportioned and developed adult figure about 1.65m to 1.68m tall.

Size	6	8	10	12	14	16	18	20	22	24
Bust	78	80	83	87	92	97	102	107	112	117cm
Waist	58	61	64	67	71	76	81	87	94	99cm
Hip	83	85	88	92	97	102	107	112	117	122cm
Back waist length	39.5	40	40.5	41.5	42	42.5	43	44	44	44.5cm

If the business of deciding on your size is impossible for you, consult someone who is an experienced dressmaker; she will be able to take a couple of measurements and sum up your pattern size by looking at your frame size.

12
SEWING TERMS

You will come across a number of words that are commonly used to describe specific points in sewing. Here is a list of those that are most often used with explanations as to their meaning.

NAP

Many fabrics can only be used hanging in one direction due to the pattern design. Others have to be used in one direction because when viewed the other way they appear paler or darker, examples being velvet, corduroy and others with surface pile. This pile is called *nap* and for the sake of convenience when fabric is referred to as being 'with nap' or 'without nap' we accept it can mean all fabrics that must be used in one direction. You will find nap referred to on the instruction sheets that accompany paper patterns.

ONE WAY

Fabrics that have a design or surface interest running the length of the fabric in one direction only. Often used as an alternative to nap.

BALANCE MARKS

Also called notches these are marks at the edges of printed paper patterns shown as triangles or diamonds. They indicate where pieces of pattern should meet when put together in fabric. These marks are also used to indicate other activities, for instance you may see on a pattern the instructions 'gather between notches'.

Balance marks or notches can be marked on the fabric either by cutting the fabric outwards in the shape of a triangle, or by marking a tiny snip in the edge, or by marking it with chalk or fabric pen.

ROULEAU

A narrow tube of fabric that is used for ties, bows and loops and buttons. Cut a strip of fabric on the cross as for binding, fold it wrong side out and machine along it with a slight zig-zag or stretch stitch. The distance between the stitching and the fold should be about 6mm. Turn the rouleau right side out using a rouleau needle.

WRONG SIDE – RIGHT SIDE

These expressions are used to describe each side of fabric, to make it clear which way pieces should be put together, which side stitching is worked, and so on. The side of the fabric that will be the outside of the garment is the 'right side'. The inside is called the 'wrong side'.

EASE

This word is used in two ways. First, patterns for garments are made bigger than body measurements in order to allow for style features and movement and this is called 'ease'. Secondly edges of fabric to be joined as seams may be of slightly different length and yet they must be made to fit together. This excess length on one edge is called ease and it will usually be marked as such on a pattern. Places where ease can be found include the tops of sleeves, shoulder seams, yoke seams and any curved seams.

BULK

Bulk is created by having two or more additional layers of

fabric under the garment. These layers are usually seam edges and if they are left untouched will create a ridge which will spoil the appearance of the garment.

The layers must be trimmed using small scissors, each one is trimmed to a different width, the narrowest one being 3mm, and unless the seam is quite straight the edges must also be snipped or clipped. This is done with the points of small scissors. All layers are cut in towards the stitching at an angle so as to reduce fraying and to help to avoid accidently snipping too far and cutting through the stitching. The snips should be made at intervals of 1cm along all curves.

Note that it is easiest to trim first and then snip.

TRIM

See above.

SNIP

See above.

GIVE

This word is used to describe elasticity in fabric. Knitted fabrics 'give' in all directions. Woven fabrics 'give' when pulled at an angle of 45 degrees and some give a little when pulled across the width. It helps to remember that use can be made of 'give', for example when cutting fabric to make strips to use for binding.

CASING

A double layer of fabric produced either by folding over the edge of the fabric or attaching an extra piece on the wrong side to form a slot through which ribbon, elastic, drawstring, cord etc., can be threaded. Casings are often used on necklines, bags, waistlines etc.

BINDING

A method of finishing the edge of a garment which involves

encasing the edge in a narrow folded piece of fabric, allowing the narrow fabric to be seen on both upper and underside. Binding is also the word used to describe the narrow strip of fabric itself.

SHAPED FACING

The term describing the piece of fabric used as a facing on the shaped edge of a garment. The garment edge may be curved, angled, scalloped etc., and one edge of the facing is cut to exactly the same shape so that it is easier to attach it and roll it to the underside of the garment.

RAW EDGE

Any cut edge of fabric is described as raw. On some fabrics these edges will fray or ravel, on others they may curl up. If they are to be concealed inside a process the instruction is usually to trim them down so that both these tendencies are controlled.

FACING

This is a method of finishing the edge of a garment. It usually involves attaching a narrow piece of fabric to the outside of the garment and rolling it onto the wrong side until it is out of sight. The edge is then said to be 'faced'.

All-in-one facing
Fold-back facing
Joined-on facing

All these expressions refer to positions where a section of garment is cut with an amount of hem to turn back that is in excess of the usual amount and it is turned to the inside of the garment and finished as a facing rather than a hem. Such garment edges are straight and cutting them with the facing attached eliminates the necessity for a seam. Positions where all-in-one facings might occur include buttoned edges, pocket tops and bottoms of short sleeves.

FACE

Sometimes used with reference to the right side of the fabric. An instruction may read for instance, 'with the sleeve face-uppermost'. Face-cloth is a type of fabric with a brushed or hairy finish on the right side.

STITCH DENSITY

A phrase used to describe how spread out or how close zig-zag machine stitching is. For example the stitch density of buttonholing is high while that of zig-zag, used for neatening a raw edge is low although the more a fabric frays the higher should be the stitch density in order to control the fraying.

13
SEWING TECHNIQUES

The sheet of instructions that accompanies a paper pattern will show you how to arrange the pattern pieces on the fabric ready to cut out but it will not tell you how to actually cut it. It will show you how to join fabric together again, but it will not tell you that it has to be pressed! There will be no tips on setting in sleeves, or zips, or hems or sewing on buttons. Follow the instruction sheet but use this book to provide the extra detail that, as a beginner, you need to know. Some of the basic processes that you will learn on other simple garments are included in the instructions for the easy garments in this book, others are listed below. Use the hints in conjunction with paper pattern instructions.

SEWING ON BUTTONS

Where to use: for holding tabs in position; for decoration, sewn right through instead of with a buttonhole and in conjunction with some of the other fastenings that follow, also, obviously, for repairs.

Buttons must be sewn to two layers of fabric plus interfacing if possible.

(a) Mark the position with a chalk cross.

(b) Thread needle with double thread – a fairly long piece – and put a knot in the end.

(c) Wax the thread by running it through beeswax a couple of times, then holding the knot between thumb and forefinger let the thread lie across the palm and using the other palm, twist the thread. Do this by rubbing one palm across the other. Wind the few inches that are twisted round the thumb, holding the knot, and continue until you reach the needle.

(d) Make a stitch on the chalk cross. Make two more stitches, stabbing right through all layers of fabric and passing the needle up again each time.

(e) Cut off the knot.

(f) Slide the button on to the needle and sew on taking the needle into and out of fabric in one movement (a). Next pass through the hole in the button, then once more pass needle through button and in and out of fabric in one movement. It is vital for button to stand away from fabric so with each stitch lift the button to be sure there is a shank. This method of sewing is a great help in forming a shank.

Length of shank must equal total thickness of piece to be passed over the button, so it varies. It is not advisable to use a matchstick or other aid because that produces a shank of only one length.

(g) Work plenty of stitches but not so many that the centre of the button looks bulky.

(h) Finish with needle and thread between fabric and button and wind thread round shank, starting from base and working to button, then winding down again (b).

(i) Pass needle several times through fabric at base of shank, pass needle to wrong side and fasten off.

PUTTING IN A ZIP

There are several ways of putting in a zip but the following is the simplest one for beginners.

Turn in 1.5cm on each side of the opening and tack near to fold.

Press, taking care not to stretch the edge.

Place the zip in position so that one folded edge extends slightly more than halfway over the teeth. The tab should lie slightly below the fitting line.

Tack through fabric and zip tape, working from the top of the zip to the bottom. Repeat on second side and then join the two fold edges together with an oversewing stitch to prevent them being drawn apart by the final stitching. This is particularly likely to happen if you are going to sew in the zip by machine.

Machine or hand stitch from the right side so that the stitches will lie down the centre of the zip tape. The best result is obtained by stitching from top to bottom on both sides, but not across the bottom as this can cause a bubble in the fabric.

Use a zipper foot if sewing by machine, adjusting the position carefully. Use a medium-size machine stitch. If you prefer to stitch by hand, use prick stitch. See page 42.

SETTING IN SLEEVES

A sleeve with gathers over the top is not too difficult to set in but you may have trouble with a plain one. The secret is in the way the fabric is held.

Complete the garment as far as you can, including finishing cuffs and sleeve edges and even the dress hem and fastenings as well if you like.

Getting the right sleeve into the right armhole

1. Lay the bodice on the table. You will see that the front of the armhole is more scooped out than the back.
2. Fold both sleeves along the seam and lay them down. You will find that one edge is slightly more scooped than the other. This is the front of the sleeve.
3. Place each sleeve to its armhole, scooped edges together and put a pin to hold the sleeve to that side of the bodice.

Set in the underarm section

1. Lift bodice and arrange armhole in front of you with underarm seam in the centre.
2. Unpin sleeve and place sleeve seam to this underarm seam. Note that you are working with right side out on both sleeve and bodice.
3. Pin the seams together and then pin a few inches of the underarm seam. Both edges are roughly the same shape so it isn't too difficult. Pin for about 7cm on each side of the central pin, just until the sleeve head begins to change shape.
4. Tack this underarm section and fasten off tacking.
5. Pin and tack second sleeve in the same way.

Having tacked the underarm, pull the bodice over the sleeve head so that the bodice is inside out and the sleeve head is indeed wrinkled up. Take the armhole and sleeve head in your fingers and roll them back so that the sleeve head is now on top.

Pinning and tacking the sleeve head

1. Ease the centre of the sleeve head back to meet the shoulder seam of the bodice. You may have transferred the dot on the pattern at that point, but it doesn't matter too much if you haven't because you can see the centre as it is flat for about 5cm. In addition to this you will be trying on the sleeve, after which it may need altering anyway.
2. Place one pin at this point, across the seam line, picking up only a very small amount of fabric on the pin.
3. Spread your fingers out under the whole area and begin to pin the remainder, dividing and subdividing each half of the sleeve head, inserting more and more pins to break down the excess fullness into such small bumps that none will form a pleat when stitched.
4. You will probably have to move the pins several times before you are satisfied. A general rule is that there will be slightly more towards the front of the sleeve where the shoulder bone protrudes than at the back where the body hollows.
5. Tack with small stitches over the pins. You may like to tack from the bodice side at this stage to ensure a good armhole line.

Stitching in the sleeve

When you are experienced you will machine the sleeve but for now thread the needle with waxed double sewing thread, work from sleeve side and stitch sleeve in using a half back stitch. Work carefully over the areas of fullness, making sure no pleats appear. Remove tacking.

You can back stitch the sleeve head to control the fullness and then put work under machine and stitch right round armhole, from the sleeve side.

Pressing

Use a pad or rolled up towel, push it into the armhole under the sleeve head and press the join with the toe of the iron. Use a steam iron or a dry iron and damp muslin cloth. Both turnings should be pressed into the sleeve to support the sleeve head. Do not press underarm except to press the actual stitching, the sleeve and bodice should hang down together under the arm.

DARTS

Darts nearly always appear in pairs on a piece of garment so they must be exactly the same size and length. Mark the size on the wrong sides of both layers of fabric with a tracing wheel and pale-coloured dressmaker's carbon paper or with a chalk pencil or fabric pen.

Fold the fabric wrong side out and match up the lines. Slide the layers and look at the cut end until you can see they are level. Put in a pin across the dart. Smooth out the fold until the point to the dart is right on the fold. Put in another pin. Tack the dart on the line, starting at the open end and tacking to the point. When you are competent you will be able to omit the tacking. Tack the other dart to match.

Run the iron lightly over the fabric then mark the points of the darts with chalk or pencil, making sure they are equal in length. Place the fabric under the machine foot with the fold on the right and the foot angled along the tacking. Reverse then stitch forward, slowing down as you reach the point exactly on the fold at the point and reverse. Take out tackings, trim thread ends, press the stitching flat then press the dart to one side with the fabric opened out.

CUFFS AND WAISTBANDS

These techniques are similar and can be handled in the same way. The easiest method for both is using light Fold-a-Band for cuffs and firm Fold-a-Band for waists.

Cut the length required ie, two pieces for cuffs that equal the paper pattern you have or one length for a waist that fits you and allows for at least 7cm to overlap. Press the Fold-a-Band to the wrong side of your fabric lining up the central perforations on the straight grain or stripe etc., on the fabric. Use a damp cloth with a medium-hot iron. When cool cut out round the edge allowing 1.5cm all round cuffs and allowing an extra 1cm all round the waistband.

Attach cuffs and waistbands as detailed on your pattern instruction sheet, pulling up the gathers or arranging the tucks etc., to fit the length of Fold-a-Band, using the edge as a guide for stitching cuffs and the perforations as a guide for waistbands. Also remember a further tip as follows. You will find it easier to cope with cuffs and waistbands if you arrange to have an equal amount of overlap at each end, rather than all at one end as your pattern probably describes. The advantages are that the ends are easier to stitch and turn and that you don't have to worry about getting the overlap at the correct end.

TIPS

When machining a long seam lift the two pieces of fabric so that they are horizontal and level with the bed of the machine and hold them slightly taut to help get a straighter line of stitching.

Always follow a routine: set up the iron, prepare the table or put out the cutting board, get out the sewing box.

While you are making something keep it on a hanger between sessions and hang it where you can see it to encourage you to get on with it and not forget about it.

When working from a paper pattern leave the instruction sheet lying about so that you can look at it between sewing sessions. You'll find you will get on quicker when you do sew because the sequence will be in your mind.

Thread up the machine well before you need it, even the day before. Sew a few stitches on a piece of fabric folded double, to make sure it is threaded correctly.

Having done some machine stitching press it with the iron, it will smooth out the wrinkles and make it look much better.

Always use thread that is a perfect match for the fabric; stitching will show less. A shade darker will usually result in a perfect match.

Always practise on double fabric, it lies flatter.

If the machine has two speeds keep it on minimum while you are learning and when you have top stitching to do.

Learn how to make your machine sew one stitch at a time so that you can stitch accurately to a given point. On some machines you can press a button, on others a quick touch of the foot control will do it, on basic machines turn the balance wheel towards you.

If the stitching does not look right, remove bobbin and reel of thread and thread up again.

To mark two layers of fabric with tailor's chalk mark one piece then put it against the other layer flat on the table, bang sharply and when you part the layers you will have identical marks on each.

Tailor's chalk can be used safely on the right side of the fabric; it brushes off.

Stand up for cutting out and for tacking.

Keep pins well away from pattern edges.

The difference between a home-made and a professional look can often be due, not to the standard of sewing, but to the skill with which the iron is used.

When you have made something satisfactorily make it again in a different colour, maybe for someone else.

Sew in pairs or small groups to help you through the areas of no confidence.

Leave your sewing out in corner of the living room or kitchen. It will tempt you to do a little now and again and you will get in some practice as well as make progress. You can hem a pair of cuffs or take out some tacking while the potatoes cook.

Handle fabric as little as possible; avoid patting and smoothing with the flat of the hand. Use only your thumbs and fingertips for touching, lifting, placing etc.

Prepare the pattern and cut out then have a break – a cup of tea – an hour doing something else – or leave it until the next day and start again.

Sew in short sessions; plan to complete one technique at a time.

Try buying ready-cut-out kits by mail order; you make a quicker start on the sewing.

Remove ends of thread and snips of fabric and fibre from

your sewing by blowing them away rather than by using your hand.

Take pins out as you come to them; drop them straight onto a magnet or into the pin box.

Use a well-matched thread – your stitching will show less.

While making something keep the scraps of fabric in a pile ready to use for testing stitching.

When putting away your pattern put in a scrap of the fabric with some machining on it to remind you of what you did next time you use the pattern.

Cut off thread ends close to the fabric at the end of each row of stitching otherwise you will have to do it again later.

Keep a 2-3cm paint brush with your machine for brushing out fluff.

Use buttons with only two holes, they are easier and quicker to sew on.

FURTHER READING

Andrews, Christine, *Embroidery for Group Working*, Dryad Press Ltd.

Butler, Margaret G., *Clothes – Their Choosing, Making and Care*, B.T. Batsford Ltd.

FitzRandolph, Mavis, and Fletcher, Florence, *Quilting*, Dryad Press Ltd.

Heafield, Margaret J., *Young Dressmaker*, B.T. Batsford Ltd.

Ladbury, Ann, *Dressmaker's Dictionary*, B.T. Batsford Ltd.

Ladbury, Ann, *Dressmaking with Basic Patterns*, B.T. Batsford Ltd.

Ladbury, Ann, *Guide to Simple Pattern Cutting*, B.T. Batsford Ltd.

Ladbury, Ann, *Improve your Dressmaking*, B.T. Batsford Ltd.

Ladbury, Ann, *Short Cuts for Busy Dressmakers*, B.T. Batsford Ltd.

Lucking, Peter, *Sewing Machine Handbook*, B.T. Batsford Ltd.

Musgrave, Belinda, *Blouses, Shirts & Tops*, B.T. Batsford Ltd.

Snook, Barbara, *Learning to Sew*, Dryad Press Ltd.

Stevenson, Amanda, *Batsford Book of Practical Dressmaking*, B.T. Batsford Ltd.

SUPPLIERS

Mail order

Mode UK Ltd 650 Holloway Road London N19 Tel: 01-263 3617	*Luxury fabrics, catalogue with swatches, write or telephone to order*
A. Garstang & Co Ltd 213 Preston New Road Blackburn Lancashire	*Silks, cottons and others, SAE for patterns and details*
Butterfly Silks Union Mills Lower Union St Skipton BD23 2ND	*A wide variety of lovely silks at various prices, send SAE*
Sussex Silks Ltd Oaken Wood House Horsted Keynes Haywards Heath Sussex	*Lovely silks, send SAE for samples*
Harlequin Lawling House Manningtree Road Stutton Ipswich, Suffolk	*Buttons and belts covered in your fabric, SAE for order form* *Also haberdashery by post*
Sari Fabrics Ltd St Mary's Road Leamington Spa CC31 1LY	*Cut and sew kits, send for details*
Hilaine Ltd Grecian Mills Bolton Lancashire	*Sewing machine tables and cabinets, send for brochure*

INDEX